The Chetwynd Chronicles

My father went out to Florida in the eighties and settled at Fruitland Park to grow oranges. He called a small district in that neighborhood "Chetwynd."

— Brian Chetwynd-Stapylton

The Chetwynd Chronicles

The British Colony of Lake County, Florida
1882–1902

D.R.S. Bott

Clowder Publishing

Clowder Publishing

Copyright © 2013 by D.R.S. Bott
All rights reserved, including the right of
reproduction in whole or in part in any form.

Designed by Sallie A. Kautz

ISBN 9780615780566

For my friend Jeni who, nearly to her last day, pushed, cajoled and shared my curiosity about the Colony of Chetwynd.

Table of Contents

Foreword

TRAVELING TO Disney World and Orlando today it is difficult to imagine the hardships faced by those nineteenth century settlers who sought to tame and develop the land.

One cannot but feel amazed when you read about the exploits of this young, aristocratic Englishman, Granville Brian Chetwynd-Stapylton, who typified so many of his generation during the reign of Queen Victoria.

He traveled to a corner of Florida where he and his partners set about the development of citrus orchards and founded the town of Chetwynd. He then went on to found a church, which still exists, and even helped to divert a railway to serve the interests of the area. As if this was not enough, Granville managed to marry, start a family, obtain American citizenship and found a bank. All this before he was 30 years old.

D.R.S. Bott makes a sterling effort to tell the story of a pioneering spirit who strove to leave the world a better place. Granville and his partners showed fortitude and determination in the face of great hardship. These are the traits that built an Empire and made America great.

Alan Chetwynd Gillett
Great-grandson of Granville Brian Chetwynd-Stapylton
Cape Town, South Africa

Preface

CURIOSITY OFTEN gets the best of me. As a parish member I'd heard from time-to-time that Holy Trinity Episcopal Church in Fruitland Park, Florida, was founded in the 1880s by young British orange growers who lived in a local but strange sounding colony called Chetwynd—pronounced *Chet 'wind.* While researching another history project, I developed an irresistible impulse to uncover all I could about the Colony of Chetwynd, the driving force behind the place, and those who lived there.

As a family historian for nearly 35 years, I first sought information usually found in local libraries and newspaper archives. To my dismay scant histories and newspaper articles, even those written in the 1920s when memory might have been sharper, proved inadequate, confusing, and often inaccurate. Further, no local newspaper archives exist that cover the period from 1882 to 1902—the years this book chronicles.

Countless hours of digging through the public records of Sumter and Lake Counties, resources available at the Leesburg Heritage Society, the Lake County Historical Society, and on the internet, finally enabled me to, like a mosaic, piece the story together. Enriching the story to a great extent are portions of letters penned by a colonist, Robert Francis Edward Cooke, along with photographs—many not previously published.

This book is written in two parts. Part One contains the narrative. Part Two is the result of a quest nobody has ever attempted to do: to identify those who lived in the Colony of Chetwynd and then to add biographical substance beyond only their names.

Perhaps you've already noted the symbol of the goat head that I've incorporated throughout the book. It is the Chetwynd crest—"One who wins through politics rather than war." After locating this image I discovered a similar crest on an 1888 Holy Trinity Church advertisement for a priest that I had previously overlooked.

Encouragement for me to write this book came from many: friends and neighbors, golf partners, and strangers I met while seeking information. I appreciate each of them and their interest in the project.

There are specific others I wish to thank who were so incredibly helpful: Susan Richmond, my editor with the critical eagle eye; Kareen Rashelle and Emil Pignetti who craftily enhanced nearly all of the old pictures; Patti Taylor who drew the area map; the gifted Sallie Kautz who designed and formatted the entire book; William Stokes who reviewed the final copy; R.F.E. Cooke (posthumously) whose letters to his father allowed me to generously sprinkle the text with anecdotes and information (read more about Frank in Part Two); Beverly Pignetti who, early on, cranked a microfilm reader and read from extremely light film at the University of Central Florida while I recorded notes; Russell Casson who, as we trespassed, walked me down to the shore of Zephyr Lake so I could get the *feel* of the area; Gail Morris, of the Lake County Historical Society, and Gloriann Fahs and the staff of the Leesburg Heritage Society for their assistance and patience; Diane Gibson Smith, the town clerk of Fruitland Park, for making photographs of the period available to me, and my most capable research assistant, *Google*. Of course I would be remiss not to thank my very fat cats, Tom and Jerry, who always managed to settle in for a snooze right in the middle of my research notes. Their fur-faced cousin, Missy, was much more thoughtful. But most of all thank you, dear reader, for your interest in this fascinating piece of local history.

Prologue

ORANGES AND LEMONS came to Florida with the Spanish explorer Juan Ponce de Leon in 1513. Grapefruit, a relative latecomer, arrived in 1806—courtesy of the French Count, Odet Philippe, who planted the first grove of grapefruit near Tampa in 1823. Around that same time, Florida established a citrus business in north Florida—chiefly near St. Augustine.

Citrus trees, in general, grew wild throughout many of Florida's forests. The story goes that orange-eating Indians who dropped seeds behind them may have been the source of trees growing here and there among the pines. Some cultivated orange groves could be found along the St. John's River and around Tampa—usually as home landscaping. Florida's unique sandy soil and sub-tropical climate proved ideal for growing the seeds that early settlers planted. Yet it took nearly 400 years from the time citrus was first introduced to Florida until enough was grown to turn it into a lucrative industry.

The so-called backbone of Florida, Sumter County—a portion of which would become western Lake County in 1887—was dotted with groves of trees bearing bright, sweet and succulent golden fruit that, when produced and marketed en masse, would lead to prosperity beyond one's wildest dreams—or so land companies of the early 1880s claimed.

That compelling claim was loudly noised abroad. Young

Granville Chetwynd-Stapylton of London, England, heard that noise and succumbed to Orange Fever. So in the winter of 1881 he bade his family and homeland goodbye and within a few weeks found himself pioneering in the densely pine-forested frontier of Sumter County, Florida.

This enterprising 22-year-old gentleman began to acquire not only land holdings all over the area, but relationships with local land companies as well as with significant individuals—in particular with Orlando P. Rooks who, in 1876, founded nearby Fruitland Park. Because Rooks had already cultivated citrus groves, he, along with two others, managed to persuade the Florida Southern Railway Company to establish a freight route to carry the fruits of their labors north to the *New World* and potentially to the *Old World* as well.

In the meantime, Stapylton built a citrus learning center of sorts at nearby Zephyr Lake where some groves already existed. Additional groves would be planted by Stapylton's British-born pupils or apprentices, as they were sometimes called. Although a few of the recruited pupils were married, most were young bachelors who came to live and to learn all aspects of the citrus culture.

Some eventually bought their own land and became fruit growers. Some pursued other interests and occupations. Some lacked the stamina or grew impatient with the time required to produce profitable crops. Some had little or no money. Some were simply homesick.

Even though social clubs, horse races and weekend night activities in nearby Leesburg kept them occupied in their spare time, the life-style was completely foreign, different, and challenging. Hurricanes, severe droughts, epidemics, economic depressions, extreme heat and devastating freezes threatened their very existence.

Consequently, most of the men and their families lived in the Colony of Chetwynd for only four to five years before moving on.

As for young Stapylton, he eventually married, helped to establish a church, continued to buy and sell land, and then entered the world of banking and finance. It was he who, with a Manhattan attorney, established the first bank in nearby Leesburg. Because of his much-publicized successes during extremely hard times, Stapylton became prominent among his Florida banking peers, as well as among the local political establishment. In 1902 he was elected Leesburg's mayor. Had he not died later that year, one wonders what his accomplishments might have been.

The Colony of Chetwynd had died a few years earlier. Disastrous freezes during the winters of 1894 and 1899 that obliterated the citrus industry for years, proved fatal. All interest in or settlement of the British colony ended.

What follows then is the only story ever written about the Colony of Chetwynd, of its developer, Granville Brian Chetwynd-Stapylton, and of those who lived there.

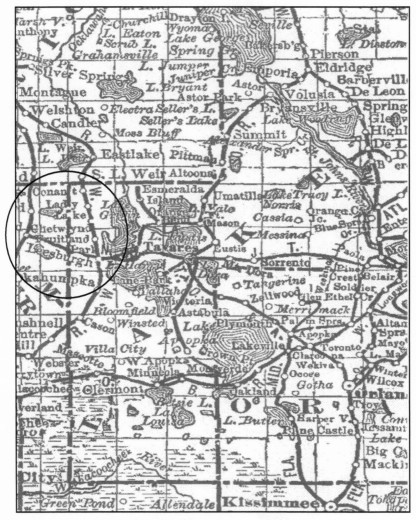

Lake County, Florida 1888

Atlas of the World (Chicago, IL: Rand McNally & Co., 1888

The dark black lines indicate railroad tracks.

Part One

Chapter One

A Not So Sunny State

THE END of the Civil War left Florida's economy in shambles. Only Virginia suffered more. Although the State's role in the course of the war was insignificant, beef and pork, food products, salt and cotton shipped to troops earned Florida the acclamation, "the breadbasket of the Confederacy."

Before the war 61,000 slaves, nearly half of Florida's population, accounted for 85 percent of cotton produced—Florida's major industry. When slaves were declared free, once wealthy plantation owners tried desperately to restore prewar production levels by hiring former slaves. Their attempts failed for two reasons: tenant farmers and sharecroppers who claimed their lands, and the inability of getting cotton bales to market. Most roads and railroad tracks had been destroyed. Many white folk

Working an orange grove, circa 1875.
State Archives of Florida, *Florida Memory,*
E. A. Abbey

fled to Brazil or to settlements west of the Mississippi River while central Floridians sought refuge in south Florida.

The decline of cotton production, however, was offset by the demand for lumber for building and re-building in the aftermath of the war. Cattle-raising and large-scale commercial agriculture then took center stage. Talk of cultivating citrus for profit on a grand scale waned. There were no slaves to pick the ripened fruit—estimated by reconstruction surveyors to have been 20,000 wild oranges annually. By the mid–1870s, however, the commercial production of citrus, especially oranges, began to rise.

Leesburg's founder, Evander Lee, migrated to the area in 1857 and settled in the woods between Lake Griffin and Lake Harris. While clearing and preparing his land to grow cotton and sugar cane, trees bearing round, golden fruit were discovered. "My grandfather did not know what this fruit was," wrote his grandson, J. Chester Lee, "but he ordered his laborers to leave the trees standing. Later, they became the basis for his first orange grove developments."

Some years later Evander Lee shipped his first ox cartload of oranges in flour barrels that were hauled to Silver Springs and then loaded onto a steamer for the journey north via the Ocklawaha and St. John's Rivers. Writing in the 1920s, a Leesburg pioneer, E. Wilson Kaler, recalled that Lee ". . . had no trouble in selling them and returned home with a bucket of money. That sale gave great impetus for a local orange industry. People began putting out groves all around Leesburg."

Fruitland Park's founder, Orlando P. Rooks, built his home on Crystal Lake in 1877. There he not only established a nursery containing rare flowers and plants such as olives and pineapple but is said to have nurtured over 100 citrus varieties. Nearby, Evander Lee's brother, John Calvin, owned a twelve and one-half acre grove, later known as the Wever Grove, that became a show place for prospective town residents.

But even as interest in the production of citrus grew, Florida needed revenue, economic stimulus, and most of all, people. Tourists from northern states, eager to escape the winter weather and doldrums, came in droves. Hubbard Hart ran paddle wheel steamboats on the Ocklawaha River from Palatka (and later from Jacksonville) to Silver Springs, one of Florida's first tourist attractions located near Ocala in Marion County. A normal year's business is said to have been 50,000 tourists a year for the two-day trip. Although tourists boosted the economy for a few months, most chose not to live in Florida the year around. Those who did often were those seeking solace in what one writer of the period called, "The grand sanitarium for the whole country."

The *Tuskawilla* on the Ocklawaha River.

Wanted: People

To encourage permanent settlement, the 1882 Florida State legislature created a State Bureau of Immigration in Jacksonville to induce individuals and families from both the United States and Europe to make their home in Florida. An important component, railroad expansion, so crucial to the development of commercial and residential areas, was well underway, especially along Florida's coasts—thanks to the two Henry's, Plant and Flagler. Passenger trains, however, would not come into being for a few years.

Land companies popped up in nearly every county. Promotional literature promising inexpensive land, profitable crops and improved health rolled off the presses. Florida's railroad companies got into the act by running advertisements in London newspapers to promote the vast interior lands available for growing all sorts of crops and cattle ranching.

Greedy land speculators dispatched their agents to England to sell the "Florida Dream," based upon the concept of growing citrus as a cash crop capable of producing an income in excess of a whopping $10,000 per year upon maturity. While it was true that land from the State of Florida and the railroads could sometimes be bought for as little as a dollar an acre, fraud, deception and exaggeration ran rampant.

At the same time ten limited liability companies (limited liability for shareholders) that held thousands of Florida acreage, registered in London to do business in Florida. In addition, a number of London agencies offered to help settlers get to "The Riviera of America," as one agent described Florida. But when efforts to entice individuals and families failed to produce the desired results, the focus shifted to the establishment of European colonies or settlements as a group.

The Notion of Colonies and the Pupil System

Some colonies were established in South Florida, but little else is known of them except for a Danish colony in White City, St. Lucie County; a Swedish settlement near Miami, and a Scottish one at Ormiston on Sarasota Bay.

At least five English colonies developed in Central Florida around the notion of an instant community: Narcoossee; Runnymede; and Aston, located in then southeast Orange County; Fellsmere, in present Osceola County; and East Hope, location unknown.

The idea of settling people of the same nationality who spoke the same language and shared the same customs would insure, it was thought, that residents would stay permanently. In addition, building some of the comforts of their homeland— schools and churches, for example—around a town center would help them feel at home.

Although Chetwynd's developer eventually sought to develop a small town in the British Colony and was instrumental in forming a church that was not in the town, his approach to developing a colony, if that ever was his original goal, took a different approach.

Chetwynd's young settlers, many of them university graduates and sons of English landed gentry, and most of them bachelors, usually came alone. Nearly all came as students to learn the citrus culture, buy some land, plant groves, and eventually make a lot of money.

At first most students were recruited by the developer's agents in London, Messrs. Ford, Rathbone & Co., who according to their prospectus operated ". . . a private Firm, independent of all land companies and agents. They have a complete organisation on both sides of the Atlantic, which ensures a thorough fulfilment abroad of every engagement entered into here. The Firm commenced operations at this office [London] in 1880."

In their prospectus the agents wrote further: "Florida is celebrated for the production of the orange, grape, melon, peach, and other fruits. A training at any of the stations provided by us for pupils qualifies them for settling in any part of the United States, Canada, Manitoba, or the [British] Colonies, where free lands are to be had; and their judgment in selecting a favourable locality for operations will be much assisted by the experience gained in their course of tuition."

Arthur Montifiore, an English explorer and author, wrote an article in an 1890 edition of England's *Macmillan's* magazine that enlarges upon the value of the pupil system.

> The majority of young Englishmen who migrate to Florida do so in the capacity of pupils. They go to some orange or fruit-grower, who boards, lodges, and teaches—in other words, works them. I have noted the pupil-system with some care, and I am of opinion that in spite of its defects it justifies its existence. Numbers of young fellows go out to this State who are too young to start on their own account, and in any case too inexperienced to be allowed to do so. In any new country experience is worth money, and this is especially true with regard to Florida. An average lad picks up a lot of useful knowledge in a year, and he at least learns what chiefly to avoid in buying land and rearing crops.

Wrote the developer in 1884: "Messrs. Ford, Rathbone & Co. . . . are the Agents for placing pupils with us, and will furnish pamphlets, etc., upon application. Further information can be obtained on arrival at New York at the Company's Offices, 19 Park Place, Rooms Nos. 25 & 26."

I am, dear Sir,
Yours truly,

G. C. STAPYLTON

Chapter Two

The Vicar's Son

How can I make you acquainted, I wonder? Above middle height, [5'8"] straight and square, fair hair, blue eyes, small fair mustache, a handsome face with a grave expression and altogether of an aristocratic appearance, and no wonder, for this family trace their descent from before the Conquest. He is rather quiet to outsiders but I don't find him so.

[Elizabeth Chetwynd-Stapylton, March 1, 1886]

I T STRETCHES one's mind to believe that the mastermind behind the development of a British Colony—ultimately called Chetwynd—near the northwestern border of present Lake County, Florida, was a young, ambitious, and energetic English entrepreneur and pioneer of dogged determination, Granville Brian Chetwynd-Stapylton.

Granville Brian Chetwynd-Stapylton

Stapylton, the youngest among four siblings, was born December 11, 1858, to William, and Elizabeth (Tritton) Chetwynd-Staplyton. Given this surname it is not surprising that the family is found in *Burke's Peerage,*

Baronetage and Knightage, a major royal, aristocratic, and historical reference book. Granville Stapylton descended from Sir Brian Stapleton (1320–1394), one the the first Knights of the Garter. The hyphenated surname became legal when Granville's great-grandfather, Major General Granville Anson Chetwynd married Martha Stapylton. By Royal License, he changed his surname to Chetwynd-Stapylton.

Granville's father, William, was the long-time vicar of St. John the Baptist Church, Old Malden, Surrey, England, an affluent village southwest of London.

There the Stapylton family lived in the vicarage that today is part of the St. John's Conservation Area. The character of St. John's, according to the Conservation Office, is summarized as "the medieval village centre containing the Saxon church, the site of the vicarage, and the 18th century Manor House."

The church itself is mentioned in the *Domesday Book* of 1086, a survey of individual land-holdings and land values in England and Wales that was commissioned for William I (William the Conqueror). In

St. John the Baptist Church,
Old Malden, Surry

1611 the church's old flint walls were repaired and the nave and tower rebuilt.

Under Vicar Stapylton's tenure, a new nave, chancel and vestries were built followed by the installation of steam heating and gas lighting. A turning circle for coaches was located in the south garden. All of the structures are located near a rapid stream called Hogsmith, a tributary of the Thames.

That the Stapylton family, according to the 1881 English census, employed a cook, a "parlourmaid," a housemaid, and a coachman, one might suppose a rather genteel lifestyle. But with four children born within a span of five years, it is not likely that all was sweet and calm. Ella, the oldest, was followed by Frederick, Edward, and then Granville. Edward, who became a wine merchant, was the first of the boys to marry.

The Rev. William Chetwynd-Staplyton

Although his father was an Oxford graduate, Stapylton chose prestigious Haileybury and Imperial Service College in Hertford Herts, where, as an honor student, his interests were geology and drama. In 1876 he won the prize for elocution—the art of public speaking.

After graduation Stapylton worked as a commercial clerk for a colonial broker in London—then the world's largest city, the capital of the British Empire, and the global capital of finance and trading.

A colonial broker was one who arranged for the import and export of colonial goods to and from the British colonies. In addition, a broker handled money transfers for the various transactions and discounted purchases by one firm or person against sales by another. In that sort of environment and as a broker's clerk, Stapylton no doubt heard about or at least read the tantalizing literature about the profit potential from orange growing in the frontier of Florida's interior. And so, as Stapylton's son Brian succinctly wrote decades later, "My father went out to Florida in the eighties . . . to grow oranges."

On the Orange Frontier

Accustomed to the hustle and bustle of Victorian London, Stapylton must have been stunned if not overwhelmed when the last steamer of his long trans-Atlantic journey—the one that carried him down the twisting and tortuous Ocklawaha River—finally slipped into the Lake Griffin dock in early December 1881. It was then that he found, as he later wrote, "The condition of life colonial with unbroken pine forest, without road or railway."

Given the urban sprawl of today, it is difficult to imagine that central Florida could have been so primitive. According to an 1880 Florida population distribution map, there were two to six inhabitants per square mile living in Sumter County. The *Florida State Gazetteer,* published in 1881, cites only 100 of the 4,686 Sumter County residents as fruit growers. At that time a mere 200 people populated Leesburg, five miles to the south,

Main Street, Leesburg, Florida, circa 1880.

while nearby Gardenia/Fruitland Park[1] was still in its infancy.

Undeterred by first impressions, Staplyton bought land almost as soon as his feet touched the fertile sandy ground of Sumter County. Given his young age (22), one wonders if he had the personal financial resources to wheel and deal in land transactions, as he ultimately did, without substantial backing.

Records indicate that he was not associated with any of the limited companies registered in London to transact business in Florida. Perhaps his London employer or his agent, business associates, or family members backed him financially.

One of Staplyton's most significant purchases occurred Wednesday, February 22, 1882, when he bought 80 quality acres on Skillet Pond—later to be called Zephyr Lake—for $2,200—from John Henderson Tanner and his wife, Louisa. This acreage represented one-half of the land the Tanners had been granted by the United States November 20, 1875. Tanner, a freed slave from South Carolina, was a beneficiary of the May 20, 1862, Homestead Act that President Abraham Lincoln signed into law. That Act entitled anyone who had never taken up arms against the United States government, including freed slaves, to 160 acres—for a small filing fee. The purpose of the Homestead Act was to encourage settlement across the uninhabited parts of the nation, including the peninsula of Florida.

Stapylton had tasted the refreshing sweetness of an orange. He had convinced himself of the potential of great fortunes to be reaped nationally and perhaps even internationally. Now he owned land with citrus-bearing trees. The land that wasn't cul-

---

[1] Because there was already a town in Florida called Fruitland, postal authorities refused to recognize Fruitland Park as the town's name although the Southern Railway Company did. From 1884–1888 Fruitland Park mail was sent to and from Gardenia.

tivated would quickly be cleared and facilities built to accommodate and train future British citrus growers. But shipping citrus to market was tedious and slow. Barrels stuffed with oranges had to be loaded onto ox carts and then transported by barge from Lake Griffin, up the Ocklawaha River to the St. John's River, and then reloaded onto a steamer in Palatka for the journey northward. Although fourteen railroad projects covering 750 miles had been completed in Florida, there was no railroad service conveniently available for Stapylton and other local citrus growers to speedily get their crops to market.

Chapter Three

Putting the Pieces in Place

L OCAL HISTORIES claim that early in 1883 Stapylton and Orlando P. Rooks, Fruitland Park's founder, a horticulturalist (cultivates plants) and a pomologist (cultivates fruit) of some renown, took two major steps to bring a railroad to the area. They, along with Rook's brother, William, and Francis X. Miller of Gainesville, allegedly gave 160 acres in Fruitland Park to the Florida Southern Railway Company. Then they hired a civil engineer, George A. Long, to design a route from Ocala in Marion County and through Fruitland Park, instead of through Dead River (east of Leesburg) as planned.

While Stapylton no doubt had more than a casual interest in re-routing the proposed track, public records do not substantiate his donation of Fruitland Park land for the project. He did, however, sell a right-of-way through his property north of Fruitland Park—for one dollar.

Eventually, persistence and persuasion to re-route the line from east of Leesburg to the west worked to everyone's advantage. The company gave in and changed their minds. Work began on a three-foot narrow gauge freight line from Ocala in June 1883. From there it went south through Conant, Lady

Lake and four miles later reached Fruitland Park, December 30, 1883. Ten days and four miles later it reached Leesburg. The first passenger train, the *Pine Knot,* rolled through Fruitland Park Sunday, January 20, 1884. Within a year the line became known as the *Orange Belt Route.*

Now there was a means of not only providing a faster and more direct way of shipping citrus to the packing houses in Ocala for shipment to Palatka and beyond, but for transporting investors and potential students and residents to the colony that was beginning to develop.

A passenger train leaves Fruitland Park.

The Zephyr Lake Complex

Except for a small piece of land Stapylton sold to Augustus P. Bosanquet on the northeast side of Zephyr Lake, Stapylton owned the east half of the land surrounding the lake that today is bounded on the south by Cooke Drive—probably a sandy, rutted trail at that time. Previously known as Skillet Pond, if measured by area, 23.5 acres, Zephyr Lake was, and still is, a pond. The town of Fruitland Park's northern boundary then, Miller Road (County Route 466A), was about a mile and a half to the south.

In addition to his 80-acre purchase from Henderson Tanner, Stapylton bought another 140 acres south of Cooke

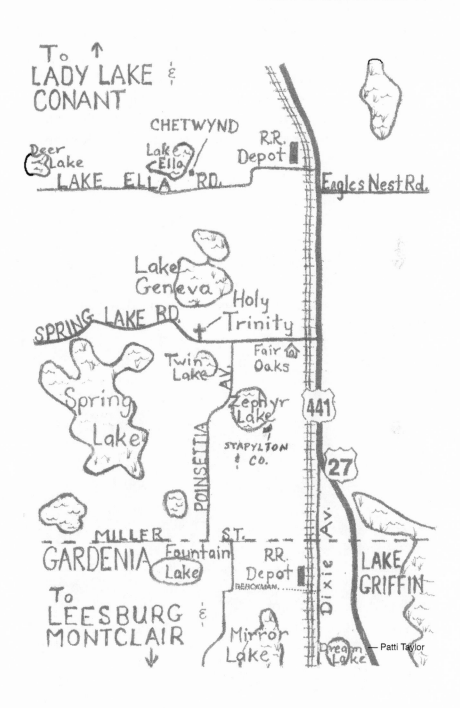

To ↑
LADY LAKE &
CONANT

CHETWYND

Deer
Lake

Lake
Ella

R.R.
Depot

LAKE ELLA RD.

Eagles Nest Rd.

Lake
Geneva

Holy
Trinity

SPRING LAKE RD.

Fair
Oaks

Twin
Lake

Zephyr
Lake

441

Spring
Lake

STAPYLTON
& CO.

POINSETTIA AV.

27

MILLER ST.

GARDENIA

Fountain
Lake

R.R.
Depot

BERCKMAN

LAKE
GRIFFIN

Dixie Av.

To
LEESBURG &
MONTCLAIR
↓

Mirror
Lake

Dream
Lake

— Patti Taylor

Drive from Douglas and Kate Lowe of Cook County, Illinois, in April 1883. That acreage was contiguous to the land bought the year before and was probably where additional groves were planted. Over the next couple of years, Stapylton sold 137 acres of his 220 total acres, including several ten-acre lots on the northeast side of the lake. The first two lots were sold August 7, 1883, to Joseph William Hannah and to James Routledge, Stapylton's future brother-in-law.

Nestled on the southeast side of the lake a complex that included a stable, a boarding house, and a dining hall with an annexed kitchen, was built for prospective young bachelor students to room and board. The dining hall was commonly called *The Hall* or sometimes *Zephyr Hall*. A single tree, aptly stripped of its bark, served as *The Hall's* center beam. Mahogany flooring was probably imported from England.

Zephyr Lake Compound, circa 1886.
Left to right: Stable, boarding house, dining hall with attached kitchen.

It is likely that the construction work was similar to that of Augustus Bosanquet's two-story eleven-room home nearby that was constructed about the same time. Land was cleared and a portable sawmill set up on the premises to use the lumber from the fallen trees.

All of the structures were built of sturdy yellow pine. Augustus Bosanquet's great-nephew, Gershon, asserted that because wood was so plentiful only the inner core of the pine tree was used; the rest was thrown away. The center, full of rosin, was believed to deter termites.

Stapylton's first home, shared with Cyril Herford, was located on a 1.35-acre plot that also included *The Hall.* Before Stapylton married in 1885, he built a home for his bride on five acres nearby.

Stapylton's first home next to *The Hall.*

The facilities and private homes were all sufficiently set back from the water to minimize the onslaught of various

From his home Staplyton could see the Bosanquet's stable and groves.

bugs, particularly mosquitoes and midges—known today as "no-see-ums."

Student Recruitment

Stapylton's first London agents, Messrs. Ford, Rathbone & Co., were replaced in August 1885 by William James Green, 8 Delahay Street, London, England. It so happened that Green and his two sons stumbled upon Stapylton's development while touring Florida and spent the summer of 1885 on site.

According to the prospectus, *English Colony, Fruitland Park, Sumter County, Florida,*

> We take pupils on the following terms for any period, from three to twelve months, at the rate of £100 [$486][2] a year, payable quarterly in advance. For this we provide board, lodging, washing

[2] All pound to dollar conversions cited herein are values of that specific year.

and instruction against an express understanding on the part of the pupil to aid diligently in the work of the orange groves and to do his work faithfully under our direction. For his labor we pay him $5 per month, and if he seems likely to make himself useful we increase this to $7.50 and subsequently to $10 a month. This monthly wage is quite sufficient to keep him in tobacco and other small luxuries.

In a March 26, 1886, interview with the *New York Herald*, Green said, "My usual way of proceeding is that when a young fellow comes to me and says he is going out I advise him to go to Mr. Stapylton's for three months and not to bind himself for a longer period, though he will probably wish to stay longer to get the experience of the whole agricultural year. R.F.E. (Frank) Cooke, age 21 and a recent Cambridge graduate who arrived in June 1886, believed that a three-month instruction period was long enough. He favored the benefit of on-the-job training with more experienced growers.

Who the instructor(s) might have been is speculative. Stapylton's lakeside neighbor, Augustus Bosanquet, already a successful fruit grower, and his Fruitland Park friend, Orlando Rooks, probably had the most local experience with citrus cultivation.

Until the June 30, 1885 Florida Census, it cannot be determined how successful student recruitment might have been. That census indicates that some of the men, all listed as farmers, batched together in individual homes after completing their training:

George Elin 21, and Villiers Smith 20
Wilfred Western 27, and Harold Trome 31
John Back 30, and Alex Creery 22
Harold Topham 29, and Edwin Topham 28
Granville Stapylton 27, and Cyril Herford 19
Francis Cosens 19, and Sydney Cosens 15

Hugh Budd 29, and Charles Hill 28, each lived in separate dwellings near the Cosens brothers. The next census entry for a single dwelling, probably the boarding house, lists:

Kenneth Streatfield 20, and J. L. Laugharne 22
John Ogilby 31, G. Sutton 19, and T. Young 30

During his visit that summer William Green observed that "about 30 students were in or around the house." He went on to admit, however, that although he was not the only agent operative in England, "not many" settlers had been sent out.

By this time twice a week mail delivery gave the colonists not only news from home but kept them apprised of world events including their own colony.

Early in February 1886 the colony became aware of an article in the *New York Herald*. A London correspondent, via a cablegram to the newspaper, claimed that Stapylton had lured his students and others to buy and ". . . to settle down on useless land and endeavor to make a livelihood from it." The men were indignant about the damaging nature of the cable and the accusations made against Stapylton, as well as the 45 men (not all of them British) who had purchased land. February 6, an angry letter was penned defending Stapylton as an honorable and trust-worthy man. "We have not been duped; we have not been misled. We judged for ourselves previous to purchasing." Thirty-four men signed the letter. (See Appendix).

The following month Agent William Green was interviewed which seems to have settled the dust-up. "Mr. Stapylton's land consists chiefly of high, rolling pine lands of first class quality. Everyone in the colony has the greatest esteem for Stapylton. Nothing could be more loyal than his way of treating the settlers," he said. The *Herald* concluded that, upon seeing Stapylton's prospectus and pamphlets, along with Green's responses, "the unvarnished truth is given."

Chapter Four

Maximum Culture Shock

W HILE THEY may have been hooked by the promise of all the money to be made from growing citrus and more than eager to make it, it had to have been an extreme culture shock for the young men who left the comfort of their families and homes across the Atlantic to risk living and trying to earn one in such a rugged, primitive, and undeveloped area of Florida—an area once called, rather appropriately, Mosquito County. It's unlikely that any of them had ever experienced tropical heat or had dealt with threats of yellow fever and malaria; ferocious storms and torrential rains or the severe lack of it. Or the danger and the reality of hard freezes like the one in 1886 that killed most of the young trees, followed by another in 1889; the variety of irritating bugs, or the big and small wild animals like bears, bobcats, wolves, deer, pigs and panthers that roamed the land, ate their crops, and sometimes even threatened their lives. It's a sure bet that few, if any, of the colonists had ever encountered alligators.

"This is a nether region," wrote Cambridge University graduate Frank Cooke, to his father, George, back home in Norwich shortly after his arrival in 1886. "Because of it we have not been obliged to adapt civilized manners such as wearing coats and ties at dinner."

For an educated, well-heeled Englishman to settle in a "nether" land required strength of character and physical fitness not to mention unlimited stamina to keep going when the going got tough. A sense of humor helped too. As one writer wrote, "The weaker fail, the stronger migrate, and the rest do the best they can."

"Well," wrote Cooke, "everything out here is a speculation." He went on to write in July 1886, "This colony is at present too poor to go in for many luxuries."

R.F.E. (Frank) Cooke

Cooke, who penned frequent letters to "My dear father" and always closed them, "Your affectionate son, Frank Cooke," wrote of long days, of often getting up at 5 A.M., and "of not a moment to spare."

A Typical Day

Clad in a white flannel shirt, gray flannel trousers and untanned leather boots, the first chore of the day was to round up, feed and milk the stock. Milk, Cooke wrote, sold for $.12 1/2 a quart. Next, suitable pasture had to be found for the cows—in Cooke's case three miles east near Lake Griffin. At one point he tried to sell some of his own herd, but had no takers. So he threatened to turn them loose into the woods—a common practice then.

Some pastures, however, were fenced. "One of our ladies, 6 feet 2 inches, was tossed over a fence by an infuriated cow, fortunately not one of mine. Luckily she was not much damaged," wrote Cooke.

There were chickens to feed and their eggs to sell. One day Cooke wrote of having to "run up" more fowl and chicken houses. Chicken droppings provided good fertilizer for orange trees. It was a common practice to keep chickens in the grove in movable pens formed like hurdles that were about ten feet in height and moved every few days. "We started with 300 [chickens] and now have 4 dozen which I think is at least 36 too many. Would almost give them away to get rid of them," he wrote. Early one morning he had to be up by 5 A.M. ". . . to sulfur all of our fowls and the houses as an unfortunate fowl was discovered with lice."

Next it's breakfast time. "Young fellows, who in England have only got out of bed at five o'clock in the morning by accident and who have never done two hours work before breakfast, find this stock-feeding a marvelous whet to the appetite," wrote author Arthur Montefiore. A typical breakfast consisted of coffee or tea, eggs, an accompanying dish, and stewed fruit.

After breakfast and a discussion about the work of the day, all hands turned out to the grove or to the garden. It was common to grow vegetables not only in a designated garden but between the citrus trees. Whether the garden or the grove, plowing was often necessary because of the clumping nature of the soil. Compared with a farming plow, the type used for citrus was so light that it could be guided with one hand. But sometimes a mule assisted.

Maintaining a grove wasn't hard work except in the summertime heat. Work stopped from about 10 a.m.—when the typical breeze came up—until four p.m. or even later. About four hours of work a day kept a grove in perfect condition.

From noon to late afternoon the men rested or kept busy

Working a Stapylton Company Grove.
Left to right: Alfred Stanley, George Back, and Mesey Fellows.

with carpentry projects or other things that demanded their attention like mending clothes or darning socks. In one letter Cooke asked his father to send him some light medium brown angora wool to darn his socks. When the late afternoon storm cleared the air it was back to the stock. After dinner the evening was free for recreation and relaxation. No one worked on Sunday.

Cooke wrote in the Spring of 1886 that there was talk of having a dance but "they can't get it up before Lent. So it is to be postponed till Easter. It's a great nuisance that Lent should come just at our best time of the year."

Occasional dances and *germans*, a cotillion or party for complicated and intricate dancing, were held at the Lake View Hotel in Leesburg.

Of a local concert Cooke wrote, "People not very critical but they relieve the monotony of things in general." In January

1889 there were two circuses, two theatricals, and a minstrel show in Leesburg. There was also a club house for English men on Magnolia Street in Leesburg that was formerly one of the old hotels. While that may sound appealing and a tad cultural, a Saturday night in Leesburg often resembled a cowboy town complete with heavy drinking, brawling, and gun fights. Little wonder that the Woman's Christian Temperance Union, an organization concerned about the destructive power of alcohol, formed in Leesburg during the 80s.

For the orange grower summer is the time of work while the fall is a period of rest. Oranges are usually ripe and ready in October; the last crop ships in May. During the winter the oranges are clipped from the branches, sized, wrapped, packed (up to 150 boxes per day), and marketed. Once done, all work in the grove itself is over for a couple of months.

Most of the men took advantage of the down time to explore Florida or to visit family back home. Cooke visited St. Augustine, Silver Springs, sailed on the Gulf, and went with Francis Cosens to Brooksville for what Cooke described as "the great Democratic meeting to select a member for Congress. Happily it passed off very quietly, as pistols were only drawn twice during the proceedings."

Cooke seemed almost blasé about a potential kerfuffle—perhaps it was a common occurrence. During the 1891 Democratic Convention in Leesburg, Stapylton found himself involved in a serious and fiery election debate. Someone drew a gun and threatened to shoot but was quickly disarmed.

Of the young men, Lillian Vickers-Smith, in her 1924 edition of *The History of Fruitland Park*, wrote "They were a happy, care-free group, upon whose shoulders responsibility rested very lightly, and they added much to the pleasure and gayety of what otherwise might have been a dull existence in the new and untried country."

Cooke, however, was eager for his own land to not only grow citrus but to farm as well. To his father in July 1886 he wrote:

> I suppose I ought to be looking out for a grove or land for a grove. Do you think if I put £200 [$972] into the land and kept my other £250 [$1,220] for contingent expenses that would do? If possible I shall try to find a place that has been started. At any rate the older the better.

> I shall be able to get one of a very large size but the clearing and planting and then *waiting* takes such a fearfully long time that only the Methuselah of the place can hope to make much out of it and no doubt their grandchildren will help them. I wish I could get hold of a good sort of fellow with about the same capital as myself with whom to go partner. I think we could manage well together 1st by buying a first-rate place and 2nd by greatly reducing all current expenses. Two men together can live very well more cheaply than 2 separately. Besides there would be the extra man's labour on the place. It is very difficult to give any definite idea of the cost of land. It varies so greatly, position being one of the chief things. A lake frontage, for instance, at a premium.

Out on His Own

Cooke's desire for his own place materialized when Villiers Chernocke Smith sold eight-acres, some already with groves, near Spring Lake to Cooke and Alfred Stanley January 27, 1887, for $320. Cooke chose the wrong partner; he was not well pleased. Of Stanley, Cooke wrote his father six months later:

> You asked me about my partner Stanley, and so I may as well tell you right here that I have been very disappointed in him, and I certainly made a mistake when I joined him. He appears to take no interest in the concern. In fact he sleeps at the Leesburg Hotel and drives out (or doesn't as the case may be) every day. We certainly have an arrangement by which, if either of us doesn't work

himself he has to pay someone to do so. This works all right to a certain extent only it's rather disheartening to know that if I don't interest myself in doing the business no one else will. [Harold] Dawn the fellow with whom I used to batch with before is here working for us and he certainly makes up for Stanley's deficiencies and we get on very well together. Socially Stanley is all right but I should prefer him being some one else's partner. Perhaps when we are really shorted he may begin to interest himself in things more. But when that will be I don't know. When we do what I think we ought to make it pay. We have a large number of poultry and eggs that are always in demand. And I think we shall sell all the milk we want.

Frank Cooke and Alfred Stanley's Dairy.

Heat and bugs took their toll on Cooke. "I am becoming alarmed. The temperature is 102 degrees; it was 82 at midnight. The house is now hermetically sealed against insects so that we can sit still in comfort on the porch. We have been living for the last few weeks on corn and cabbage salad," Cooke wrote in July 1887. He was learning that summer lasts well over five months in Florida rather than five weeks in England.

March 9, 1888, Cooke purchased Stanley's half interest in their property for $300. An amateur photographer, Cooke built a darkroom, set out a flower garden, ornamental trees and shrubs, established a lawn, harvested peas, beans and strawberries, and grew tangerines, grapefruits and oranges. After a freeze in March 1889 he wrote, "Everything looking so horrid after the frost. All tender things killed back and looks black, brown and white."

Within a year, however, he wrote, "Orange trees in full bloom, strawberries and mulberries ripe, blackberries and peaches in bloom. [Cooke sold peaches for five cents a quart.] The thermometer being just now, 100 degrees in the shade, I have hung up my photo of the icebergs in a conspicuous place; it is a pleasant and cooling picture in this weather."

George Winter, who was privately educated by an English priest, was according to a family historian, ". . . sent to Florida after his aunt paid a premium to a Mr. Stapleton [sic] to take him as a pupil" in March of 1886—a couple of months before Cooke's arrival. By 1888, Winter had purchased 60 acres on Picciola Island on Lake Griffin.

Winter wasn't feeling too optimistic when he wrote his mother, Maria, during the Christmas holidays:

> I don't think that I would ever do anything at orange growing as it wants some capital to start, something like £100 [$487] a year for ten years, then a grove would begin paying. It is like most things, it wants some capital and a lot of energy and the one I haven't got and the other is very scarce. I am learning the blacksmith's trade which I hope will come in useful to me somewhere.

According to James William Gambier, the managing director of the Florida Land and Mortgage Company, "There is a long, hungry gap between raw pine woods and groves of bearing orange trees [five to seven years]. It takes many hard licks, plenty of pluck, assured health, good luck and favorable auspices."

It didn't hurt to have a convenient store close by either.

Linville & Company

About 1884, Asahel W. Linville, a Quaker from West Chester, Pennsylvania, and a partner of the Keystone Brick Company in nearby Whitney, Florida, opened a general store, a stock company, near Spring Lake. Its location was convenient for the men living at Stapylton's compound as well as residents in the general neighborhood.

February 2, 1888, Cooke wrote:

> I have bought 3 shares in the store here from George Back. It is a company originally formed by 10 men each with a share at $100. The shares were afterward raised to $150 at which they are now. Co. [Company] reduced to six. Back buying 2 men out got the extra share at $175 each. I gave Back $525 for the 3 which I think was a fair price considering the past dividend just paid nearly 50 per cent besides which a percentage is returned to each partner on his purchases reducing them thereby to cost price. The firm trades under the name of Linville (one of the Co.).

James Routledge managed the store for a few months following Linville's death in November 1889. Then the stock was sold to colonists A. Mirrielees, F. C. Older and A. G. Foote who moved it to the Clark building in Fruitland Park in 1890. A massive fire on Christmas Eve that year forced them out of business.

Chapter Five

All the Queen's Horses . . .

B EFORE THERE was a semblance of rutted sandy roads suitable for a horse and buggy, trails just wide enough for a horse and rider wound their way through the woods from town-to-town and place-to-place in the earliest years of the colony. Aside from walking, horses were the primary means of transportation; most of the settlers owned at least one. To accommodate the students' horses, along with their saddles and harnesses,

The stable at Stapylton and Company.
Note groves in the background.

a large stable had been built on Stapylton's Zephyr Lake compound.

Of the six-mile ride to her wedding reception in December 1885, Elizabeth Stapylton wrote, "I shall never forget the bright picture it made, looking back at any turn in the road, to see the whole cavalcade streaming through the trees, the horses of all colours, their riders most of them fine-looking men with their white riding breeches shining in the sun."

It is doubtful that any of the young men brought horses with them. They did, however, bring horse racing with them —a Sunday afternoon pastime they thoroughly loved and enjoyed—as riders and as spectators. Like today the horses had colorful names like Pharoah, Castor, Lady Bird, Bob, Glu-Glu, and Johnnie Long Tail. Although it can be assumed that not all, if any, of the men owned thoroughbred horses, breeding of them was already a profitable business in Marion and Alachua Counties to the north.

Frank Cooke snapped the June 1887 picture below of the

Hurdle Race.
Left to right: Claude Strachey, S.H.V. Willis, William Trimble,
Alfred Stanley, and George Elin.

hurdle races. Hurdling is a form of steeple-chasing that is less physically demanding of the horses. The obstacles consist solely of hurdles one to two feet lower than the obstacles on a steeple-chase course, and the races are normally less than two miles in length. "I think the hurdles are the most interesting as it shows how a horse jumps," Cooke added. The preceding picture was taken at a track on Picciola Island. It is obvious that the track bore no resemblance to Astor, the world's most famous race course back home, located near Windsor Castle.

Pearl Stallings, daughter of Jesse and Lenora Mathews Stallings, lived on Lake Griffin's Picciola Island and recalled to a reporter decades ago, her experience of the last race at the track there. About five miles east of Zephyr Lake the race track was located on or near the island prop-erty now owned by the United Methodist Church's Life Enrichment Center. As the story goes one had to ride through shallow water to get to the track.

Miss Stalling's aunt and uncle, Margaret and Reuben Mathews remem-bered another race track a mile west of Lake Ella on Sand Mountain Road when talking with local his-torian, Loren Stover, several

The trail to Picciola Island.

decades ago. Now Lake Ella Road, it is located about a mile

north of Zephyr Lake. Pearl Stalling's grandparents, David and Nancy (Davis) Mathews lived nearby as did a skilled horseman, John Ogilby.

The American British and Colonial Racing Association

"Capt. [John] Ogilby one of our colonists died rather suddenly last week from a chill caught in surveying the Race Course. He was the originator of the Races and so it seems rather hard that he should die just a week before the 1st races of the new ABC Association [American British and Colonial Racing Association] of which he was President," Cooke wrote February 6, 1888 .

Apparently there was an old ABC Association that organized March 15, 1887, at Picciola with races also at Montclair in May 1887, according to captioned photographs. (Montclair was located west of Leesburg.) But it wasn't until November 21, 1887, that The American, British and Colonial Racing Association filed articles of incorporation with the Florida Secretary of State. A May 31, 1888, Lake County deed indicates that the

Ogilby's picnic, Picciola Island, March 15, 1887.

Tropical Florida Railroad Company sold 80 acres to the American, British Colonial Racing Association for $100. This acreage was located southwest of the town of Montclair—currently bounded by Flatwoods Road on the west and Youngs Road on the south—about five miles south of Zephyr Lake. The association—R.F.E. Cooke, president; George Webster; and E. E. MacKenzie—sold this land December 16, 1915.

A series of photographs, dated in 1887 and 1888, are captioned with the name of the race, the horse's name and their riders. Riders noted are Alfred Stanley, Henry Elin, Eugene Bosanquet, Robert Cowen, Cyril Herford, Alex Creery, Frederick S. A. Maude, George Elin, Thomas Vincent, Claude Strachey, S.H.A.V. Willis, William Trimble, H. L. Laugharne, R.F.E. Cooke, R. G. Shepherd and Francis Cosens.

The grandstands comprised ladies and gentlemen, either standing along the fence, or standing next to or seated inside their buggies and carriages—at least one of them an Omnibus

The grandstand at Picciola Island.

carriage, the Cadillac of carriages. Colonists Frederick Maude and his business partner, Walter Neve, sold them at their up-scale livery stable in Leesburg.

In addition to the bareback hurdles, there were obstacle races, as well as one called the Open Flat—a race primarily for three-year-olds—described by horsemen as "the pinnacle of prestige, glamor, history and money." A favorite was the Egg and Spoon race.

All riders, with a spoon in the mouth and an egg placed on it, are mounted on their horses and then evenly spaced along the fence. An announcer then asks the riders to do certain tasks, such as walk, trot, stop, reverse direction or circle. Riders can be disqualified for dropping their eggs, using their hands on either the spoon or the egg, catching a falling egg and replacing it, or not following the announcer's directions. The lucky winner is the last rider with the egg still on the spoon at the end.

George and Henry Elin's drag.

Another race was the Drag, the precursor to automobile drag racing but with horse-drawn carts.

"Correspondent" Frank Cooke won the Cheroot Stakes, generally a two mile race. Each rider, on starting, lights a cigar (Cheroot) and is to keep it lit until the finish line. They leave the starting line in a cloud of smoke.

Mule Race. Left to right: Arthur Stanley, Henry Elin, Eugene Bosanquet, Robert Cowen, and Cyril Herford.

Mule races usually capped off the afternoon's races.

True or not, local lore claims that the revelries observed at the race tracks by a visiting English priest led to the establishment of the Holy Trinity Episcopal Mission in 1886. Because the men rode their horses to church, not long after Holy Trinity's first service December 22, 1888, a fence was placed around the church acre with hitching posts on the south side. A bit later a stable was built on the northeast corner of the churchyard.

When the lych gate was built in 1889 hitching rings were screwed into the pine trees in southwest corner of the church acre along with those flanking the lych gate.

As a tribute to the young men who wore riding habits to church, until 1945 it was customary for the congregation to stand during the offertory. If sitting it was difficult to remove money from the pockets of their tight-fitting breeches.

Chapter Six

The Colony's Social Clubs

C OULD THE amenities of life in Merrie Olde England be
duplicated in a strange land? The colony's gentlemen tried
to make it so. Much has been written about their love of horses
and horse racing. But there was also a desire to stimulate their
minds, to play competitively, and to share their individual
talents. Records indicate that there was, over the years, a Painting
Club, the Moonlight Series, thought to have been for music per-
formances, and a drama group called The Chetwynd Strollers.

Frank Cooke wrote of acting in two theatricals at the club:
An Unwarrantable Intrusion and *Do You Know Me Now.* "I was
jolly in the latter piece and made a great hit by being rammed
into a barrel so tightly that it was with the greatest difficulty that
I ever got out again," he wrote.

These special-interest groups were components of two
social clubs, the Forest Club and the Bucket and Dipper Club.

The Forest Club

In 1883 George H. A. Elin established the Forest Club in
a large clubhouse built on two acres not far from the Stapylton
compound on the eastern shore of nearby Spring Lake. Club-

house amenities included a billiards room and a reading room. The Forest Club remained in existence through 1886, and perhaps until 1891 when the clubhouse (by then adjacent to Frank Cooke's property) was purchased from Elin by Cooke and Hugh S. Budd for the Bucket and Dipper Club. Dues were so high, it's been claimed, that membership waned and the club folded.

The Bucket and Dipper Club

Meetings of the Bucket and Dipper Club were first held in homes or at Zephyr Lake and then at the Forest Club. Membership, by vote of members, was exclusively for Lake County British gentlemen. It is notable that none of the British residents of Conant, near Lady Lake, were members.

Club by-laws provided for at least two meetings a year. A president who was also the treasurer, a secretary, and three committeemen were elected annually to serve as the Committee.

Meeting minutes tell of rather advanced parliamentary tactics, especially when rules were amended or entry fees discussed. Lengthy and comprehensive bylaws that included many sections appear to have been written by a committee of lawyers or wannabe lawyers. This bylaw defines the significance of the club's name:

> Section 20: At meetings of the Club whether for business or entertainment all provision in the way of refreshment beyond water with Bucket and Dipper is strictly prohibited: Provided that it shall be the power of the Committee by special leave or cause shown, to authorize moderate refreshment on any occasions.

The Committee decided what games could be played and what the stakes would be. The bylaws made it clear that all games were regulated and there was to be no gambling. Two favorite games were chess and whist, a popular, relaxing and simple card game that dates back to England in the 17th Century.

A Synopsis of Some Minutes

January 23, 1885 *Miscellaneous Evening at Tophams* [Harold and Edwin]. The program included members who played the piano, recited or read, sang, or showed card tricks. Often the men recited Shakespeare and had spelling bees.

Back row, left to right: Arthur Halford, Alex Cazalet, George Elin, Villiers Smith, Wilfred Western, Alfred Doudney, Kenneth Streatfield, Phillip Dietz, John V. Smith, Alan Smith, Charles Hill, and Hugh Budd.
Middle row: Frederick Maude, George Back, Harold Dawn, William Dunn, Evan Lloyd, Cyril Herford, and Charles Chesshyre.
Front row: R. G. Shepherd, George Dawson, William Gould, Alex Creery, George Male, Stephen Bonnett, and Thomas Vincent.

June 2, 1885 *At a meeting held on the suggestion of* [George] *Musgrave it was decided to form a club for social entertainment.* The minutes then list the 19 original members. (Appendix)

October 1885 *At Tophams on Spring Lake: another Miscellaneous Evening. Sold a curtain to the Chetwynd Strollers and authorized*

Hugh Budd to sell them props at a reasonable price. Budd lamented that he was unable to sell the make-up boxes.

July 13, 1886 The first monthly meeting. No meetings were noted for 1887 and 1888 until November 24, 1888, when it was decided to have a library and raise the entrance fee from $1.00 to $1.50.

August 14, 1886 Ladies were invited to a concert. The minutes noted that some members were absent because they had *gone to England* or were members of the Forest Club.

September 7, 1886 First quarterly General Meeting: *Proposed by K.* [Kenneth] *Streatfield that admission be charged for entertainments for the purpose of raising a fund towards buying an organ for the church.* There was no discussion; carried unanimously.

June 9, 1887 Annual Meeting at Zephyr Lake: *Comparative inactivity due 1ˢᵗ to disorganization of Committee caused by* [William H.] *Dunn's absence and large quorum demanded by rules and 2ⁿᵈ to apathy on part of members owing probably to plethora of commitments with the Church site and other Church questions,* [horse] *race meetings, picnics, shows in Leesburg.*

July 2, 1887 *G. C. Stapylton's song "Bridge of Fancy" was received with great applause and throughout the evening songs and music gladdened the ear whilst* [George] *Elin served out lemonade to assuage the thirst of the great smokers.* Attendance was small because of a barbeque in Leesburg and the first meeting of the Moonlight Series.

October 29 1887 *Met at the Forest Club for conversation.* There was a "theatrical" that year for members and about 50 guests.

Refreshments *were supplied* in the billiards room. Ice cream sold for ten cents a plate; lemonade was free.

A library was established in 1888 containing *Books of Reference, Standard Works of Literature, the Arts and Sciences, quarterly and monthly periodicals as well as any books that may be presented to the Club and accepted by the Committee.* Cooke complained that he rarely saw a newspaper because "the proprietor wants subscriptions for nothing in return." He added that the club was "practically at a standstill. "

May 25, 1889 It was reported that there had been four debates, two concerts, three whist evenings, one miscellaneous evening and a spelling bee with an average attendance of 29.

May 31, 1890 Forty members. An announcement was made that 410 books were in circulation and that *debates improved enormously.*

Debates were very popular with members; the minutes detailed all of the arguments. Topics included War and Arbitration; Abolition of the House of Lords; Mormonism; The Decadence of the British Empire; Compulsory Military Service, and Unemployed: That public water shall be instituted by the government for the unemployed of their country. A debate about Naturalization carried by a vote of six to five.

Stapylton supported Woman's Suffrage. He argued that his opponents had never used anything but old stock arguments which are as old as the hills and he declared himself in favor of giving the franchise to women on the same qualifications as men. Women would use it for their family and country, the highest test of civilization which he considered was the way in which the women were treated. But the US is the place, where all the most benevolent improvements come from women such and hospitals and nurses. A motion passed however that Suffrage was inexpedient and the application for it is mischievous.

December 27, 1890 The club decided to have a *Merry Christmas dance instead of a long and dry debate about politics. The bitterly cold wind that blew through the broken windows nearly killed all those not dancing.* Thirty-five were present and *the dancing kept up until 11:30.* The next month, after the windows were *mended,* there was another dance. *It was nearly Sunday before Home Sweet Home was played and carriages were ordered.*

In 1890 the club purchased a piano from Mrs. Sinclair. It could be rented for the cost of tuning it.

May 23, 1891, the Forest Club was leased for $135 a year.

November 14, 1891 A Social Smoker at the clubhouse. *About a dozen members present who smoked and talked but wouldn't sing as they were all too shy except for A. G. Love who obliged with "Ballyhooly"—V.* [Villiers] *C. Smith and Dudley played.* (The increasing number of smoker events seem to have coincided with the increasing production of cigars in Havanatown, located in Ocala.)

November 28, 1891 A general meeting held at *The Hall,* where members voted to purchase the Forest Club from Frank Cooke and Hugh Budd with borrowed funds at 10% interest. *G. C. Stapylton made a few remarks in which he accused the management of apathy in the getting of entertainments and said that unless they were prepared to provide better entertainments he saw no use in pur-*

chasing the Forest Club. The management (H. S. Budd) repudiated G. C. Stapylton's accusations. Applause at the close of the President's speech on the subject clearly showed that Mr. Stapylton's accusations against the hard worked officials were entirely without sympathy from the rest of the members.

Stapylton attended no further meetings.

One of the first amenities added to the permanent clubhouse was a tennis court.

Columbus Day 1892 residents of the area were treated to entertainment at the clubhouse with George Pybus as the master of ceremonies. Sarah Smith played a piano solo, Pybus, Charles Bosanquet and Mr. [F. A.] Barrett sang while John Vickers Smith and Frank Cooke played a piano duet. The program closed with *the farce and dialogue of "Woman's Rights."*

November 25, 1893 Dues for those who lived outside a four-mile radius of the clubhouse would be charged $.50 annual dues.

May 25, 1896 It was reported that a gasoline stove was purchased for $2, plus $30 for the redemption of shares, beautifying the grounds and for the painting club.

November 28, 1896 A piano committee was established to purchase a new one. During this period refurbishments were made to the clubhouse. A Water and Garden party was scheduled at the Frederick and Maria Schreiber's home. Attendance was 31.

1897: 26 members. It was decided that the club could not afford a dance.

May 25, 1901 The final entry in the minute book. A General Annual meeting at the club: Louis P. Bosanquet in the chair, Villiers C. Smith, Harry N. Cadell, Arthur G. Halford and Joseph W. Hannah, honorable secretary. No entertainments *owing to lack of talent and scarcity of people.*

Chapter Seven

Stapylton's Real Estate Interests

NOT ONLY did Stapylton acquire land with ten United States land grants, he bought many parcels of land all over central Florida. And he connected with local land agents, especially The Sumter County Florida, Land Company of which he was an officer—first as its corresponding secretary by 1884, and then by 1887, its treasurer—a position he held until 1899.

The Sumter County Florida, Land Company

The hand of the Sumter County Florida, Land Company, or at least the fingers of a some of its officers, are apparent in many of the real estate schemes that occurred in the 1880s. This company is not to be confused with another land company with a similar name, The Sumter County Land Company, an English company that held about 50,000 acres—primarily in Sumter County. Capital for the former entity which began operations in the spring of 1884 was provided by its officers:

Jacob A. Dunning, President
Mark W. Collins, Vice President
George M. Hubbard, General Manager
George Hollinshed, Secretary

John G. Herndon, Treasurer
Granville C. Stapylton, Corresponding Secretary

Except for Dunning, a Manhattan real estate broker and attorney, the officers were all Leesburg business men as reported in the *Florida State Gazetteer and Business Directory 1886–1887.* Collins and Hubbard operated the Leesburg Ice and Cold Storage Company. Hubbard married Isabelle, the sister of John Herndon.

Herndon and his five brothers, all born in Alabama, organized as Herndon and Herndon and owned and operated stores or businesses, ranging from the South Florida Real Estate Exchange to hardware and groceries to watch making and jewelry. George Hollinshed, who was listed as a land agent in the 1885 Florida Census, formed the Florida Mutual Consolidated Stock Company with his brother, Arthur, in 1886. Arthur Hollinshed lived in Conant.

According to classified advertisements in London newspapers,

> The Sumter County Florida, Land Company . . . offers selected ORANGE LANDS at moderate prices. These lands are situated on the line of the Florida Southern Railroad. Contracts taken for planting and caring for orange groves (trees guaranteed), and all improvements made at the lowest cost to ensure satisfactory results.

Conant

From its inception the Sumter County Florida, Land Company (SCFLC) focused primarily on a development near Lady Lake called Conant, which legally was in the south half of Section 8, Township 18 South, Range 24 East. (The Public Land Survey System, a rectangular system, is thought to have originated with Thomas Jefferson. Much of the land west of the

Appalachians was divided into square townships of six miles on a side and then subdivided in one square mile sections numbered from 1–36. Sections can be divided into quarter sections, quarter of quarters or irregular lots.) This area stretched east from Lady Lake north to about a half-mile south of the Marion County line or along present US Route 25.

As for Stapylton's interests there, in early 1882, the United States government granted him 320 acres in what became a portion of Conant. In April 1884, he sold some of it to the Florida Southern Railway, whose tracks ultimately divided Conant along the present highway. May 8, 1884, he sold the remainder of his land, probably representing his capital investment, to the Sumter County Florida, Land Company.

Conant was named for Major Sherman Conant, a financier of the Florida Southern Railway Company, and a former attorney general of Florida. July 14, 1884, a plat map (shown on next page) was drawn and filed. Some of the streets were named for four officers of the land company—Hubbard; Hollinshed; Herndon, and Stapylton. Commercial businesses, the Lady Lake Post Office and the Blue Parrot mobile home park have replaced those streets.

It has been written that Conant sales were handled by a subsidiary, The Conant Land Company—George Hollinshed, Jacob Dunning and James W. Speight, officers. That appears not to have been the case. Forty-nine sales in Conant were recorded in Sumter County and its offspring, Lake County, by the SCFLC. None of the deeds bear the name of The Conant Land Company. An 1899 sale was made by the Florida Mutual Consolidated Stock Company, George Hollinshed, president, and James Speight, secretary.

Most purchasers, many of means, had resided elsewhere in the United States. Among them the Charles Gomperts family

Plat map of Conant, July 14, 1884.
Plat Book 1, page 8, Sumter County, Florida.

from New York City, who were among the founders of the Holy Trinity Mission. Gomperts, had been a diamond broker turned citrus grower. Some upper class English folk, many of them retired government employees or military officers, lived in Conant as well.

Conant boasted of a luxurious 130 room, three-story hotel—James Speight, proprietor—that opened during the winter of 1884 and catered to the area's upper crust. The hotel was located on the northeast corner of Griffin Avenue (then paved with sawdust) and present US 25, directly across Griffin Avenue from the Conant depot.

A Conant resident, J. M. Walton, told in an interview with local historian, Loren Stover, that he'd counted "93 well-

Nurseryman Walter Poole sits on his mount near the Conant Hotel.

mounted English men and ladies riding from Chetwynd to Hotel Conant for New Year dinner."

Wrote William Kennedy in his Lake County history published in 1929, "Its promoters went in for snobbery and 'cut' all who did their own work or who sent their children to public school instead of a private school that was opened in Conant. It is, within any recollection, the only town that made this practice of snobbery, for the usual spirit of the communities in Lake County was comradeship, helpfulness and hospitality." None of the snooty Conant English gentlemen joined the Bucket and Dipper Club, the county's only British club. They simply had no use for commoners.

According to the *Florida State Gazetteer and Business Directory of 1886–1887,* Conant claimed 100 residents, a good hotel and graded school, an Episcopal Church[3], a saw mill and three

---

[3] The mention of an Episcopal Church raises the question of not only its location but its reality. Holy Trinity, Fruitland Park, did not exist at that

stores. "A jeweler, blacksmith, shoemaker and laundry are needed. The price of lands is $7.50 to $25 per acre."

After the Great Freezes of 1894 and 1895, some of the remaining Conant residents tried to make a subsistence living by extracting pine resin from the trees to distill into turpentine. That venture didn't last for long. In the meantime the grand hotel was dismantled, shipped to south Florida and re-built there.

Conant disappeared from Lake County maps by 1904, but it wasn't until 1919 that mail service was discontinued and moved to the town of Lady Lake. Today Lady Lake recognizes a portion of the town south of Griffin Road as "The Conant Neighborhood."

---

time, but Grace, Ocala, in Marion County, did. Grace Church established missions—one of them named St. Chad's—in southern Marion County. Missions were known to have existed, at various times and lengths of time, in East Weirs Lake, South Weirs Lake, and Weirsdale—all located in Marion County. Weirsdale's Presbyterian Church originated from the purchase of a building under construction by Episcopalians. Any one of these missions would have been in reasonable proximity to Conant but none were in the town limits. A Methodist Church is shown on an old hand-drawn Conant map.

Chapter Eight

Stapylton and Company

I N THE SPRING of 1884, Stapylton created some sort of a
loose partnership with three colonists. A couple of Sumter
County deeds recorded that year name George H. A. Elin,
Alexander Creery and Cyril Francis Herford as having had a
quarter interest each in land with Stapylton. But only Herford
is referenced in a formal partnership agreement written December 10, 1884, that names a new partner along with a name for
the partnership.

In an 18-page, handwritten, wide-ranging document—
devoid of any punctuation—is named 19-year-old Herford with
whom Stapylton had "engaged in the business of fruit and
vegetable growers and of all things appertaining to the tillage of
the soil and of dealers in land and real estate and of agents for
real estate investment in land and other businesses for some
time." Now the two men, also housemates, were admitting
Hugh Sandeman Budd, age 28, into a new partnership called
Stapylton and Company.

They agreed to "become and remain partners in the trade
of business of orange fruit and vegetable growers market
gardeners nurserymen and farmers and owners of and dealers in

lands, house and real estate and of and in all things appertaining thereto or to the cultivation use or improvement thereof and of real estate agents and agents for investment in and for the sale purchase cultivation or improvement of real estate . . . during the term of five years."

Three Estates

A schedule of holdings, valued at $10,890, comprised of three *Estates*—the *Home Estate,* the *Fruitland Park Estate* and the *Lake Griffin Estate*—was attached to the partnership agreement. The total capitalization of the partnership—Stapylton and Company—was $18,150. Their bankers were Messrs. Ambler, Marvin & Stockton of Jacksonville, and Messrs. Melville, Evans & Company of London.

The *Home Estate* was located in the northeast quarter of Section 4, where Zephyr Lake and the complex were located.

Holdings in the *Fruitland Park Estate* amounted to 16 acres—in the town of Fruitland Park—in the southeast quarter

NE1/4 Section 4 *Home Estate* 57 Acres	NW1/4 Section 3
SE1/4 Section 4 *Fruitland Park Estate* 16 Acres	SW1/4 Section 3 *Fruitland Park & Lake Griffin Estate* 157 Acres

of the same section plus 40 acres in the southwest quarter of Section 3 to the east of Section 4. Also in Section 3 was the *Lake Griffin Estate* containing 117 acres. By this time the Florida Southern Railroad tracks split the *Estates*.

Lake County tax lists from 1888 to 1900 indicate some estate land had been sold. In 1888 the *Fruitland Park* and *Lake Griffin Estate* was listed with 157 acres (117 of them wetland) and 56.5 acres—the acreage representing the *Home Estate*. The *Fruitland Park Estate* had been sold that year to E. W. Kline. By 1900 57 acres of the *Home Estate* and 113 acres in the *Fruitland Park* and *Lake Griffin Estate* were taxed.

Also documented in the schedule of holdings were "Stock and Effects: two mules poultry nursery and greenhouse plants waggons harnesses implements tools furniture linens glass crockery kitchen utensils and cutlery plus one share of one hundred dollars in the stock of A. W. Linville and Company," [the local general store].

Each of the partners was entitled to live at the *Home Estate* rent free, but not board. Their horses could also be stabled on the premises but with charges for their feed—at cost.

June 16, 1885, Stapylton and Company recorded their livestock mark and brand—S.C.O.—at the Sumter County courthouse in Sumterville. A listing for Stapylton and Company, "real estate and commission brokers and agents" appears in the *Florida State Gazetteer and Business Directory 1886–1887*.

The newly formed partnership advertised the "English Colony of Sumter County . . . constantly and rapidly increasing," in the classified section of London newspapers. They were seeking "Settlers, Investors in Wild Lands or Orange Groves, or pupils. . . ."

Herford sold out and migrated to another British colony in middle Tennessee, called Rugby, leaving Stapylton and Budd as partners. Stapylton and Company, according to county records, engaged in only 20 land transactions—the first in 1894.

July 16, 1885, a plat for the town of Yalaha on south side of Lake Harris was surveyed and filed for G. C. Stapylton in Sumter County, but the absence of deed records indicates that he never owned land there. Apparently, land ownership was not a prerequisite for platting an area. Yalaha's chief product was not citrus; it was asparagus fern. They exported a lot of it.

In the fall of 1885, Stapylton sold 1,503 acres—at least 370 of them either swamp land or wetland involving 15 separate parcels of land in various areas of the county—to his father, William, for $15,000, or about $10 per acre—roughly half the average cost per acre sold in the area at that time. Some of the acreage included lots on Lake Ella that had been platted the year before. Perhaps some ready capital was needed.

Chapter Nine

Sand Mountain: The Town of Chetwynd

S PECIFICALLY EXCLUDED from the December 1884 Stapylton and Company partnership agreement was a 120 acre sub-division, referred to in that agreement as *Sand Mountain*. Stapylton and Cyril Herford were to maintain their previous partnership arrangement in that development.

Located a little over a mile north of the Zephyr Lake compound, *Stapylton's Sub-division*, as it became legally referenced, had been surveyed July 1, 1884, for Stapylton by the same civil engineer who had platted Fruitland Park, George A. Long. The sub-division was set off into 39 lots of various acres or portions thereof, surrounding a lake from henceforth named Ella—presumably for Stapylton's only sister and oldest sibling, Ella.

A roadway 30 feet wide surrounded the lake. Sand Mountain Road, on the southern boundary of the sub-division, is now called Lake Ella Road.

Stapylton's Sub-division was located in the north half of Sections 28 and 29 and the southern half of Sections 32, and 33 of Township 18 in Sumter County. May 7, 1886, Stapylton sold, however, all of the portion of the sub-division in Section

29 to two men from New York, Dr. Samuel Smallwood and William H. Morrison. That portion became a part of the Chetwynd Land Company in January 1887 and included ten of Stapylton's original 39 sub-division lots.

The first lot Stapylton sold in *Stapylton's Sub-division* was October 29, 1885, to the Rev. William R. Cosens, the father of

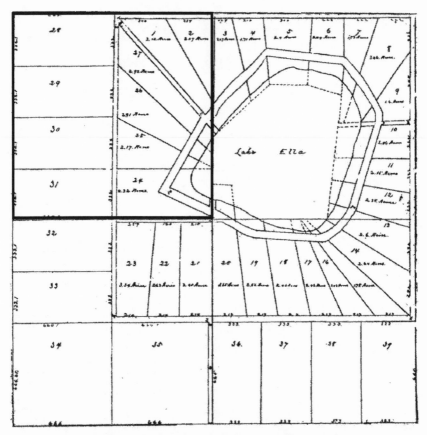

Plat map of Staplyton's Sub-division, July 1, 1884.
The northwest lots outlined were later sold to the Chetwynd Land Company.

colonist Francis Cosens, who bought Lot 12 of 2.54 acres for $101.60 and then sold it to William Morrison. Except for one sale, all subsequent sales were recorded between October 1885 to October 1886. The only sale recorded in Lake County was in March of 1888—to the Rev. Spencer Fellows, the father of Gerald Mesey Fellows, a colonist. Although Stapylton's father, William, owned 12 lots on the south side of Lake Ella that his son sold him in 1885, only 12.5 lots were actually sold by Granville Stapylton in what became known as the town of Chetwynd.

> William J. H. Ogilby of Dungiven, Ireland, Lot 3 and
> part of Lot 4
> Kenneth R. Streatfield of Morden, Surrey, England, Lot 5
> William H. Dunn of England and Patterson, NJ, Lot 6
> John Arthur Stanley and John Alex Thomas of London England,
> Lot 7
> Francis J. Mirrielus of London, England, Lot 8
> Thomas F. Gibbs of Clifton, England, Lot 9
> The Rev. Spencer Fellows of Norfolk, England, Lot 10
> Thomas H. Herndon of Jefferson County, AL, Lot 11
> The Rev. William R. Cosens of Dudley Vicarage, Worcestershire,
> England, Lot 12
> William H. Morrison of Manhattan, NY, Lot 13
> The Rev. William Chetwynd-Stapylton of Old Malden, England,
> Lots 14-20, 36-39
> William John Green of London, England, Lots 21, 22, 23

Chetwynd, first appeared on a Rand-McNally map of Sumter County in 1886.

A Holy Trinity Mission circular, *Chetwynd*, dated December 1888 begins, "Chetwynd is a new Station and Post Office (with daily mails) on the Florida Southern Railway, six miles N.W. of Leesburg." The entire context of the brochure promotes the *Chetwynd colony*, its new Episcopal mission, and the urgent need for a priest. Thus, Chetwynd was a town in the Colony of Chetwynd, unabashedly described in the mission's circular as an area of ten by three miles numbering ". . . some 80 British souls, men, women and children." In truth the colony comprised

British folk who lived on either side of the Florida Southern railroad tracks from Lady Lake to Leesburg.

Stapylton is said to have been instrumental in the establishment of a post office in Chetwynd June 9, 1887—the first in the new Lake County—formed from Sumter County two months earlier. The post office was probably near the railroad depot about a mile east in the proposed town of Dundee.

That same month Frank Cooke wrote his father, "They are building a large hotel near here at the new town of Chetwynd." Although it backed up to Lake Ella, he did not indicate the hotel's location.

The Florida Southern Railway advertised its Orange Belt route in the Florida Exposition edition of the *Florida Semi-*

The Chetwynd Arms Hotel, Chetwynd, Florida circa 1888.

Tropical News January 1, 1889. Chetwynd was named among those towns having "Fine Hotels and Ample Accommodations for the Tourist and the Invalid."

"CHETWYND ARMS,"

Opens January 1st.

SEASON 1888.

CHETWYND ARMS is six miles north of Leesburgh and about twenty-five miles south of Ocala on the Florida Southern Railroad. It is situated in the highlands of Florida, and is surrounded by a heavy growth of large pine trees. A charming lake, spring fed, lies immediately in the rear of the house. The surroundings command all that may be essential to health.

Dr. Agnew, of New York, has been on the premises and pronounces the location one of the healthiest in the State.

Chetwynd Arms is a modern building, entirely new, and has a fine frontage of more than an hundred feet, and is provided with large and roomy piazzas that almost encircle it. The interior is handsomely decorated and furnished, including Turkish rugs throughout the house. I. B Case, who has been with the St. Denis Hotel and Taylor's Restaurant for many years, begs to assure his many friends that he will give to their individual wants his immediate care and personal supervision in all that may be necessary for their comfort.

Chetwynd may be reached by rail direct from New York via Coast Line, or Steamer to Savannah, thence by rail to Jacksonville, from there via Florida Southern R. R. to Chetwynd station.

Leesburgh is just beyond Chetwynd, and our patrons are advised to purchase through tickets to that point, they can then get off at Chetwynd Station.

Further information may be obtained from the St. Denis Hotel, New York, where descriptive circulars and rates will be given, or address direct.

I. B. CASE, Manager,
CHETWYND ARMS,
Chetwynd, Lake Co., Fla

A Chetwynd Arms advertisement for the 1888 season.

The Chetwynd Arms Hotel stayed open for only a season. Chetwynd land sales had dried up long before then. Stapylton's dream did not materialize. By December 1889 Chetwynd vanished from the Florida Southern Railway's schedule. Subsequent railroad maps instead displayed Dundee as a regular stop, replacing Chetwynd.

---

48   **LAKE COUNTY.**

The main line Florida Southern Railway (J., T. & K. W. system), from Ocala, Marion County, and beyond, has stations within and near the county as follows :

	21....South Lake Weir (*Marion Co.*) 53
	24....Conant........................50 **N**
	26....Lady Lake....................48 **Λ**
	29....Chetwynd ....:45
Dist. fr.	30....Fruitland Park 44
Ocala.	34....Leesburg [1]..................40
	36....Corleys 88
	38....Helena.......................86
V	39....Okahumpka 85
S	44....Casons...... 80
	48....Centre Hill (*Sumter Co.*) 26

[1] Connects with J., T. & K. W. to Fort Mason (see p. 47); F. C. & P. to Wildwood (see below); and Lake Griffin steamboats. For continuation of this line, see p. 63.

Florida Southern Railway Schedule includes Chetwynd.

The post office re-located to Fruitland Park, December 4, 1891. Chetwynd disappeared from Lake County maps altogether after 1892.

Cooke wrote his father February 23, 1892, that there had been a big forest fire that burned three houses at Chetwynd "(including Morrison's which was a very large and costly one as houses go out here) two or 3 three shanties, three barns and stables and a few groves. All belonged to absentees. Will provide good pasture for my cows."

The last known media-printed mention of the town of Chetwynd appeared in the May 30, 1904, edition of the *Ocala Evening Star*. It reported that two sawmill men from St. Petersburg, J. F. Simpson and Will Hyde, met with Charley Marry, a Weirsdale merchant. It seems that the mill men were seeking supplies for a mill to be located in Chetwynd, "some ten miles south of Weirsdale, on timber land purchased of J. J. Tillis, the Lady Lake tie man." Tillis, of Marion County, had leased all of the timber growing in all of Section 28, except Lots 1 through 8, from Edgar and Susan Delahunt of Buffalo, New York, July 16, 1903. He sold the lease to W. A. Guthery August 16, 1904.

By March 1905, Lake County records referenced the subdivision as *Lake Ella*. John D. Robertson acquired six platted lots around Lake Ella from the tax collector for a grand total of $116.06. In November of that year Elizabeth Stapylton, sold lots 21, 22, 23, 35, (bought back by her husband) to Robertson for $50.

Over time Robertson purchased over 12,000 acres in Lake County and created the naval stores industry by building a distillery in Fruitland Park to process pine tar from its trees into turpentine. By 1913 the Lake County Land Owners Association of Fruitland Park, purchased Robertson's land. They then embarked upon an aggressive advertising campaign to attract more permanent residents to the area.

December 3, 1962, Stanley, John and Henry Denski petitioned the Lake County Commissioners to vacate that part of Lake Ella, "a subdivision, as per plat thereof filed January 4, 1892, Plat Book 2, page 16 [the same plat map filed in Sumter

County in 1884] . . . lying in the Southwest quarter of the southwest quarter of Section 28.

The resolution stated that none of the streets and roads were included in the county's or state's road systems and that they were not traveled on or used by the public. Further, the area was unincorporated. The area was ordered *Vacated*.

Chapter Ten

Decision-Making Time

IN FEBRUARY of 1885, Granville Chetwynd-Stapylton presented himself to the Sumter County Clerk of Courts in
Sumterville to make a "Declaration of Intention to become a
citizen of the United States as follows to wit:

> I G. C. Stapylton, an alien, a Native of England and a Subject
> of Queen Victoria aged Twenty Six years being duly Sworn, I
> Granville C. Stapylton do hereby declare that I am now a resident
> of the State of Florida that I have resided in the United States for
> the last three years and that it is my bona fide intention to become
> a citizen of the United States of America and to renounce forever
> all allegiances and fidelity to any and every Foreign Prince, Poten-
> tate, State or Sovereignty whatsoever and particularly to the Queen
> of the united Kingdom of Great Britain and England of whom I
> am now a Subject.
> Filed February 7, 1885 and recorded June 18, 1885.

Stapylton became a United States citizen September 12,
1896, in Tavares, Lake County, Florida.

Within a year after his arrival in 1886, Frank Cooke considered applying for citizenship. "However upon seeing the
paper I had to sign my patriotic principles would not permit my
signing it, and muchly to my credit I remain an Englishman."

Cooke, however, eventually changed his mind. He was naturalized November 1, 1901.

Although not yet naturalized, both men, as did other colonists, registered to vote in Lake County September 24, 1888.

Registered Voters of District 11

The preserved but tattered pre-1900 voter registration journals consists of columns denoting name, age, occupation, residency, and height, apparently the identifying feature. Robert A. Halford was the shortest man at five feet two while John Vickers Smith claims the title for the tallest at six feet one.

To qualify as a registered voter, one must have been a United States citizen, a resident of Florida for 12 months, and of Lake County for six months. Nearly all of the colonists listed below registered between 1888 and 1890 and all were at least 21. None of these men were naturalized (at least five-year residency) when they registered, but they paid their poll taxes, and voted nevertheless.

H. S. Budd	W. Neve
C. R. Bosanquet	G. E. Pybus
R.F.E. Cooke	A. G. Reynolds
R. Cowen	R. S. Reynolds
C. N. Chesshyre	E. B. W. Sergeant
Earl Geary	H. Allen Smith
A. G. Halford	J. V. Smith
R. A. Halford	V. C. Smith
L. L. Kenny	G. C. Stapylton
F. S. A. Maude	Geo. Winter
G. C. Muriel	

Chapter Eleven

Love and Marriage

ASIDE FROM HIS intent to become a citizen, Stapylton had other intentions too. It seems that James Routledge lived across the lake from him along with his wife, Rose, their daughters, and his two unwed sisters, Harriett and Elizabeth. The siblings were three of four children of James and Sarah Barber Routledge. Their other sibling, Emily, had married Steele Park and lived in England.

Elizabeth Routledge Chetwynd-Stapleton

In the late spring of 1885, Stapylton was smitten by Elizabeth Routledge, who was born August 20, 1853, in Haggerstone, London, England. They courted for nine months before their marriage, December 15, 1885, in the sitting room of her brother James' home. A Methodist clergyman, Isaac R. Vandewater, then living in nearby Fruitland Park because of his wife's health, officiated. The only others present were Elizabeth's local family, and Stapylton's partners, Cyril Herford and Hugh Budd. She had no bridesmaids.

A couple of months later the new bride wrote her sister, Emily:

Gardenia, Sumter
County Florida U. S. A.

3.1.1886

My dear old Embly,

I shall begin by wishing you all a very, very happy New Year in spite of all the desertions Missenden has suffered lately. [Missenden, a large town between Midlands and London, England, was suffering a severe economic depression.] You must feel dull there now, but I hope to hear soon of other people coming to take the places of those who have left.

I have two letters to thank you for besides the dear little card (what do you mean to imply by sending me those two little nestling birdies? Do you think them suggestive of a newly married couple?). Helen's handkerchief and lace. I think them so pretty and used the hanky on Christmas evening when I dined at the big house belonging to Stapylton and Co., in company with one lady and about 20 bachelors—besides our respective husbands. It does seem to me such an odd fate that I, who have lived all my life almost exclusively amongst women, should settle down in this colony of bachelors! Well, I prefer the bachelors to the old maids of Bournemouth.

I know you would like to hear all I can tell you of our wedding day. It was a wedding after my own heart—unconventional to a degree and therefore all the more enjoyable. You asked me what I wore. When anyone asked me what I was going to be married in, I told them "dark blue." So I was—in riding habit.

I had no bridesmaids and we had no fuss at all. The ceremony was performed in James' sitting room. The only people present were Rose, Harrie, James, Dolly and Granville's two partners. Granville and his partners wore their riding clothes also. As soon as it was over we joined a huge riding party of about 58 people, nearly the whole of our English colony. There were two ladies besides myself, one an American girl who with her brother were the only exceptions to the English element. It was a cold day but beautifully fine and everything looked lovely in the clear sunlight. It was such a pretty sight to see all the party beginning to move.

We started from Granville's old house where there is a large clear enclosure and you can imagine how jolly it would look to see all the horses and their riders trying to get into some sort of order. Our horses wore white satin rosettes on their bridles and we of course led the way.

We rode through the woods to Conant, about 6 miles off, where we had an informal luncheon. I shall never forget the bright picture it made, looking back at any turn in the road, to see the whole cavalcade streaming through the trees, the horses of all colours, their riders most of them fine-looking men with their white riding breeches shining in the sun and the woods perfectly gorgeous with the autumn tints of every conceivable shade of red and gold and brown and gray and green. I for one truly enjoyed it and I believe everyone else did. I felt very strange too when I heard Gran introduce me as "my wife" and was quite puzzled once or twice to know who people meant by "Mrs. Stapylton."

After lunch we rode home again, coming straight to our dear little house. You see we have been consistently unconventional throughout, even to dispensing with a honeymoon.

I do love our house so. Embly, it is so pretty and cosy and so prettily furnished. I don't know whether it would look so good to you, though, the Florida houses are quite different from those in England. Our sitting room looks to me perfect. We have a high, old-fashioned looking mantlepiece of plain paneled woodwork with open fireplace of course for log fires (I have not seen *coal* in Florida), with brass fenders and fire irons and logs. On the floor we have two lovely Smyrna [Turkish] rugs, and leading out of the sitting room is a recess which we dignify by the name of library. It contains bookshelves, a lovely writing desk, at which I am sitting now, and a chair. It has two windows with pretty little oriental looking curtains.

In the doorway between the library and sitting room, instead of a door we have a pair of beautiful curtains, deep rich crimson with oriental looking border, with dull blue and gold worked into it. All our chairs except one are rockers, and are wicker work. I hate upholstered furniture in this country, it is just a refuge for moths, silver fish, roaches, etc.

I possess two worktables, both very pretty and of Granville's choice. He is so thoughtful you would never know but what a woman had arranged the rooms when we first came to the house, he did it all himself. I am dreadfully afraid of getting spoilt and am quite sure no one ever had a kinder, better husband.

You say in your letter you feel you don't know him. How can I make you acquainted, I wonder? I think I described him before, didn't I? Above middle height, straight and square, fair hair, blue eyes, small fair mustache, a handsome face with a grave expression and altogether of an aristocratic appearance, and no wonder, for this family trace their descent from before the Conquest. He is rather quiet to outsiders but I don't find him so. I think we are something alike in some things, for instance most people think us both very reserved, excepting those who know us best.

We were engaged six months. I don't think two people ever enjoyed their engagement as we did. He came to see me every day except when he was away at the sea side, and when he was in Jacksonville buying the furniture, and on both these occasions he came back before he was expected. There was never once the faintest shadow of a doubt between us and I don't believe there ever will be. An acquaintance would never suspect him of half his thoughtfulness and gentleness, as he would strike one as being very matter-of-fact. We are both fond of reading and like the same sort of books. Altogether, I don't know what I have done to deserve anyone half so good.

We have had such lots of beautiful presents already and we are daily expecting three cases from England, containing all sorts of lovely things from Granville's friends—silver, pictures, crockery, ornaments etc. G's mother is going to give us a piano. We are just longing for all these things to come, and have two cases on their way from Australia too.

I have been frightfully busy, for besides having so much needlework to do for the house and myself, another niece made its appearance three weeks before the wedding and that made us busy over the way too. Only think of Rose with three children, the oldest only 2-1/2 years! Poor old Harrie! I don't think she enjoys the babies any more than I do. She is very well—much better than she was in England. I think it was quite the best thing for her, coming out here. We have had no wedding cake yet. It is on it's way from England! [Rose is Elizabeth's sister-in-law; Harrie her sister.]

I wonder what you would think of the life out here. One has to do so much for oneself. We are lucky enough to have a youth of 19 as a servant. I find him a real comfort. I would not be bothered with a girl servant here for anything. Would much rather do everything myself, although that means real hard work, especially in the summer. Rose had a girl out from England. She got married very soon, so James says he will import no more unmarried females, bearing in mind that I was engaged after three months.

I must finish now, dear old Embly. I don't know when Harrie will find time to write. She is as busy as I am, I think. I only wish she were as happy. The days pass like a happy dream. I do so enjoy our dear cosy home. I love pottering about over the housekeeping. We have a fine big storeroom too. Give my love to all and take a large share for yourself from your old friends.

Lizzie C-S

It seems so funny to sign my new name.

Chapter Twelve

A Church for the Colony

WHO PLANTED the notion of establishing an Episcopal Church in the colony four years after Stapylton arrived on the scene in early 1882? Was it really at the insistence of a visiting priest from the Old Country, who intended to inflict guilt upon the young gentlemen who trotted off to the race track every Sunday afternoon to engage in unseemly behavior instead of going to church? Lore says it was. Or were the services at Grace Chapel in Fruitland Park, really so "irregular" that the colonists' needs weren't met—as circulars later claimed?

Might the missionary priest there, John Baptist Caillerrier Beaubien, been too evangelical or low church to suit their worship tastes? He had that reputation; he was a popular interpreter of tongues. At that time a furor over high church (more Catholic) versus low church (more Protestant) was in full bloom in the Church of England and hotly debated, sometimes violently.

Could the "want" of a church been based upon tradition—the English tradition of anchoring an Anglican church in the center of town or in this case, an Episcopal church in the center of a British colony, so that it felt a little bit like home?

Perhaps there was simply a deep yearning and need for a spiritual dimension to their lives. No one really knows why the church was born nor exactly when.

September 2, 1888, vestry secretary Thomas A. Vincent wrote a history inscribed in the first vestry book. He wrote July–July 3, 1886. Subsequent vestry minutes recorded in 1935, declares, however, that "the third Sunday in February will from thence forward be set aside as Founder's Day with the caveat: This anniversary falls in June but since the majority of communicants have returned North by that time, it was felt advisable to have the day observed in February."

Given that assertion, along with the acknowledgment that there were seasonal members even then, June is most likely the month the notion was conceived—maybe a result of some banter around the whist tables at the Forest Club. It then makes complete sense that the church was eventually named Holy Trinity, because most years that particular major feast day in liturgical churches—the Episcopal Church among them—is celebrated in June.

So July 3, 1886, a meeting took place at "Stapylton and Company's Dining Hall" where, true to Anglican tradition and practice, a committee formed. Alex Cazalet, Thomas A. Vincent, E. Burslem Thomson, Francis R. S. Cosens, and Kenneth R. Streatfield were appointed "to work up the matter."

One might wonder if the creation of Holy Trinity Church might have been a project by the colony's developer, Stapylton, rather than a decision based upon a nudge from or, as the Church fathers might say, an "inspiration of the Holy Spirit."

Unlike today's denominational marketing standards, there is neither scriptural appeal nor the pious puffery, so common during the Victorian age of the late 1800s, in any of the church's preserved documents. But then it's unlikely that any of the young men involved had experience in planting a church. Even worse, no ecclesiastical guidance was readily available. At that time, the Diocese of Florida had neither a Bishop nor a Standing Committee to oversee the operations of the diocese and make decisions. Nor were discretionary funds available from the diocese or, for that matter, from colony residents. So it's not surprising that non-colony contributors, particularly English contributors, were aggressively solicited.

Fund-raising and Site-picking

The first invitation to subscribe to the Church Fund and to pay a priest's stipend is dated August 22, 1886. Pledges for annual support, it states, could either be submitted to G. C. Stapylton's bank in Leesburg or to their London agent, Messrs. Melville, Evans & Company—the same agent involved in Stapylton and Company's real estate enterprises.

For the next two months the Building Committee dealt with site issues that allegedly involved several contentious meetings, discussions and changes. Finally in late January 1887, it was decided to build a church on the present site, located about halfway between Fruitland Park to the south and *Stapylton's Subdivision* (town of Chetwynd) to the north—a short stroll or horseback ride from Stapylton and Company's compound on Zephyr Lake.

March 24, 1887, G. C. Stapylton, as trustee of the Episcopal Church of Florida, bought one acre of land for $20 from Samuel L. and Alice R. Tanner on which a church would be built. Apparently Stapylton didn't know that all church property is held in trust for the Episcopal Church. Although the diocese knew a mission was forming in Chetwynd, the whereabouts of the deed was not known for some time. Finally Granville and Elizabeth Stapylton sold the one acre to The Protestant Episcopal

Church in the Diocese of Florida for one dollar December 4, 1888. The purchase of the "church acre," as it became known, was now official.

With fund-raising under way and the site decision made, the first committee resigned and was replaced by a fresh one: Harold Topham, Francis R. S. Cosens, Earl Geary, and Wilfred Western with Thomas Vincent again named secretary and treasurer.

A Priest-in-Waiting

The issue of securing a priest was also front and center. Even then a priest came with a church like a horse with a buggy.

Prior to the site decision and upon a recommendation from an unnamed source, Stapylton contacted the Rev. John Campbell Wheatley Tasker of London "as a future chaplain . . . to undertake the cure." This move grew out of the committee's frustration with the newly consecrated Bishop Edwin Garner Weed's foot-dragging to appoint a priest for the new mission. Perhaps they hadn't absorbed that fact that there was a severe shortage of priests, specifically missionary priests, in the Diocese of Florida.

Sixty-one-year-old Tasker accepted Stapylton's proposal to become the priest-in-charge and arrived in Chetwynd in early December 1886. Perhaps Tasker viewed the challenge as an opportunity to also investigate Florida's moths and butterflies. He was a well-known entomologist, who specialized in Lepidoptera, the study of moths and butterflies. In memory of her father his daughter, Elizabeth, donated 13,000 species to the Harvard University Museum of Comparative Zoology in 1905.

Trivia aside, Tasker met with Bishop Weed three times that December and received permission to not only conduct the first service of the new mission but also "to undertake the duties of the district." The district, according to diocesan records, included Fruitland Park. So on Sunday the 19th at 3 PM Tasker led 50 people in Evening Prayer at the "Dining Hall at G. C. Stapylton's, ESQ." Holy Trinity Episcopal Mission of Chetwynd was officially and successfully born.

Four services were subsequently held at Stapylton's Dining Hall followed by three at the Forest Club located near Spring Lake. By January 23, 1887, services were conducted, according to Frank Cooke, in "a temporary church which is simply an old barn fitted up"—on John Vickers Smith's land (also purchased from Sam Tanner) on Lake Geneva to the north of the newly-purchased church acre.

The Vickers-Smith barn circa 1887.
John Tasker may be the priest in the foreground.

Most of the accoutrements of Anglican worship adorned the primitive barn—an altar with an embroidered frontal, brasses given by Tasker, a lectern, and substantial wooden chairs to accommodate worshipers. With English customs prevailing, prayers were probably not only offered for American civil authorities but for the Queen and the Royal Family as well.

Prepared for worship in the barn.

Seventy people attended Easter services April 10 where "according with the Rites of the Episcopal Church of England and America," the three daughters of James and Rose Jane Routledge, Dorothy, Audrey, and Brenda, were baptized—the first recorded baptisms of the mission. The girls were the nieces of Elizabeth Routledge Stapylton. Tasker, according to church service records, returned to England about three months later.

Tensions began to rise. According to the June 9, 1887, minutes of the Bucket and Dipper Club, there was "comparative [club] inactivity due to apathy on the part of members owing probably to a plethora of commitments with the Church site and other Church questions."

Since fund-raising efforts initiated the year before didn't produce the desired results, the families of the young colonists were solicited to pay for a priest. Frank Cooke was not well pleased. He wrote his father, "I was very much annoyed at your receiving a begging letter about the parson's stipend, and which I find has been sent to everyone's people without our knowledge. Think you have done quite enough for the church and think we ought to be able to keep this old parson." This indicates that Tasker may have still been on the scene.

Meanwhile Stapylton's father, William the Vicar, stepped up to organize a bazaar July 1 and 2, 1887, on the Vicarage Grounds, Old Malden, "In aid of the Building Fund of Holy Trinity Mission Church in Florida." The bazaar was in addition to a concert sponsored by his parish earlier in the year. The combined proceeds netted £367 or about $1,780. The Rev. Stapylton's efforts were so successful that he and his parish are credited with raising nearly all of the funds to underwrite construction costs.

George Winter's brother, the Rev. Charles H. Winter of London, wrote in 1955:

> I helped, in a small way, to build it [Holy Trinity]. In 1886/7 I spent time in Switzerland. We had our Services at one of the Hotels. One day a Mr. Lasker, I think that was the name, [it was Tasker] took the Service and asked help for a church he was building in Florida at Fruitland Park, that he knew George as 'the Man of the Woods' and showed me two photos. One was of an old crock he said George had killed. It was laid out on a long wicker chair and had a large straw bonnet fixed on its head [and a church-warden's pipe stuck in its mouth]. Quite a good and funny picture.

In the meantime the departure of the "old parson" left the colony without a priest. Spencer Fellows, rector of St. Mary Magdalene, Pulham, Norfolk, England, was enlisted to baptize Granville Brian Chetwynd-Stapylton October 30, 1887, the son of Granville and Elizabeth. Fellows, whose son Gerald Mesey lived in the colony, had purchased 60 acres near the town of Chetwynd a couple of years before.

The First Burial

According to Thomas Vincent, vestry secretary, the Rev. Isaac R. Vandewater officiated at the December 3, 1887 burial of James Vickers Smith, 74, formerly of London, England, and the oldest colonist, "in the church acre"—the first burial recorded in the parish register. Vandewater, a Methodist minister who lived in Fruitland Park about 15 years and helped establish the present Community Methodist Church, had presided at the marriage of Elizabeth and Granville Stapylton in 1885.

By mid-January 1888, Rowland Hale, rector of St. Mary's Church, Fayetteville, Tennessee, arrived to supply the mission for three months. His stipend was limited to each week's offerings or about two dollars at best. While serving Holy Trinity a choir, no doubt a mens choir as was the English custom, was formed along with the establishment of weekly celebrations of Holy Communion, a high church characteristic then. Stapylton's father had begun that practice at his parish about ten years prior.

Although there is no record of services from April 1, 1888 to December 2, 1888, it is likely that Joseph Ernest Julian, the new priest at St. James, Leesburg, provided occasional afternoon services.

Chapter Thirteen

From Building to Consecration

WITH ABOUT $2,150 pledged—most of it from English patrons—a contract to design and build the church was given to two Savannah, Georgia, gentlemen—John J. Nevitt, architect, and E. Thompson, builder. True to Anglican tradition, the church was built exactly on an east/west axis—the west emphasizing the external entrance into the church; the east end focusing internally. The congregation would face the east, the direction of the coming of Christ.

Land was cleared, sawmill equipment brought in, and builders hired. Construction of the yellow pine Carpenter Gothic board and batten church with the steep gables, fish scale shingles and a cypress roof rising, at its peak, 75 feet above the foundation and topped off with a bell tower without a bell, proceeded toward the goal of being ready for the first service, Sunday, December 2, 1888—nearly two years after the mission's first official service at Stapylton and Company's dining hall.

But the fledgling mission still had no assigned priest and the vestry again convinced itself that Bishop Weed was not trying his best to find one. So the three-man vestry of Stapylton, Vincent and Alexander Cazelet, all appointed by the bishop,

Holy Trinity Mission, Chetwynd, Florida

decided to place a promotional advertisement in some English church newspapers while the bishop continued to make independent efforts of his own. Bishop Weed was successful. On the appointed date, December 2, Joseph Julian, the "Episcopal minister in Leesburg," conducted the first service in the new Holy Trinity Mission, Chetwynd, Florida, to a congregation of 50. The offering was $4.96.

The Rev. Joseph Ernest Julian

Julian, who had already served the St. James Mission in Leesburg for a year, became the first rector (not called a vicar then) of the new mission. Until the mission became self-supporting with a full-time priest, finally attained in 1965, Holy Trinity would be yoked with St. James. A priest would be shared.

St. Stephen's in Yalaha, St. John's in Brooksville, and St. John the Baptist in Montclair, would share Julian too. Established in January 1888, the Montclair mission coincidentally bore the name of Stapylton's boyhood church in Malden, England. It so happened that Stapylton and Company owned and operated a nursery in Montclair and most Sunday afternoons horses raced at a track nearby.

That the interior of Holy Trinity church was not completed by the first service is not unusual. The heart pine floor hadn't been oiled nor was the vestry (robing room) for the priest furnished. There were no pews, no organ, no choir stalls nor a reading desk for the priest. Not only was there no altar rail, but no kneeling cushions for communicants. And the bell tower already leaked.

But over the next seven months quite a transformation took place. Most of the furnishings were purchased and installed, including hand-crafted pews by a Fruitland Park carpenter, Jonathan Luther, which for the next 40 years only extended halfway back in the nave—enough to seat a congregation of about 60. They were used for the first time on Easter Day 1889. "I used to like the taste of his [Luther's] pine wood pews when I was a small boy—that is when I was kneeling!" wrote Brian Stapylton, the son of Elizabeth and Granville, in October 1956.

Meanwhile, the church acre was fenced and painted with a double gate in the center of the south fence where hitching rings were also attached. A stable was built in the northeast corner of the church yard along with a shed for harnesses and saddles. Prayer books were purchased as well as a dust pan and a brush, and a rake—all in time for the consecration of the new Holy Trinity Mission, Chetwynd, Friday, July 23, 1889, at 11 A.M. "The church was tastefully decorated and the service as choral as our singing capacity admitted of. The weather tho very

Interior, Holy Trinity Mission shortly after consecration.

hot was beautifully fine. The Bishop afterwards held a reception at Messrs. Stapylton and Budd's hall."

It took three years to plan, raise funds, and build the $2,500 church. Items like chancel chairs, a baptismal font, oil lamps, and matting for the church aisle would have to wait until later.

Those identified as founders:

George R. Back
Augustus P. Bosanquet
Eugene P. Bosanquet
Louis P. Bosanquet
Hugh S. Budd
Alexander P. Cazalet
Robert F. E. Cooke
Francis R. L. Cosens
W. C. Earle Geary
Charles and Amanda Gomperts
Charles Gomperts, Jr.
Clarence Gomperts
Gertrude Gomperts
Laura Gomperts
Jonathan and Maria Josephine Luther
James and Rose Jane Routledge
Elizabeth Smith
James Vickers and Mary Smith
John Vickers Smith
Margaret Smith
Sarah Smith
Villiers Chernocke Smith
Granville and Elizabeth Stapylton
Kenneth R. S. Streatfield
Ernest B. Thomson
Thomas A. Vincent
Wilfred P. P. Western

The September 11, 1887, account of the first vestry meeting of Holy Trinity Mission, Chetwynd, lists G. C. Stapylton as the Senior Warden—a position he held until 1892. Also the lay reader, he continued in that position until 1895 when he and his family moved from their home on Zephyr Lake to Leesburg.

The Lych Gate

Curiously, no official church records account for the construction in 1889 of perhaps Holy Trinity's most significant national distinction, the lych gate. Brief historical accounts dating back to the 1920s cite the year, which has never been disputed.

The word *lych* is the Old English word for corpse and is also one of those rare words that have survived modern English. Most often found in English churchyards, a lych gate is usually made of wood, as is Holy Trinity's. Essentially, it's a roofed porch-like structure over a gate of four to six upright posts in a rectangular shape. A number of beams hold the pitched roof.

In earlier times the shrouded body or a coffin rested on staves between two benches inside the lych gate after being carried from the deceased's home.

Later, pall-bearers rested after removing the bier from a cart or hearse. Today it is common for the deceased's family to sit on the benches while awaiting the ministers to begin the procession into the church.

Holy Trinity's lych gate, which closely resembles the gate at Stapylton's boyhood church, replaced the double gate on the south side of the church acre. Because the south church entrance was used

The famous lych gate built in 1889.

nearly 75 years as the main entrance, worshipers entered the church by first walking through the lych gate.

One of the oldest, if not the oldest lych gate in the United States, it was funded by Emily Tatham, a life-long English Quaker who faithfully worshiped in the Episcopal Church. She was the aunt of Maria Schrieber, who along with her husband, Frederick, lived in the colony. Said to have resembled Queen Victoria, Emily was born in 1835 in Settle, Lancashire, England, and died in 1907 in Ocala, Florida.

The Colony of Chetwynd could now boast an exquisite church and lych gate, plus the continuing ministry of a priest. Wrote Frank Cooke, "Most of the colony are now happy and today (being Sunday) have been swaggering to church in their latest London fashion."

Chapter Fourteen

Morrison, Stapylton & Company

EARLY IN 1886 one of the Stapylton & Company partners, Cyril Herford, relocated to another British Colony in middle Tennessee, called Rugby, so Stapylton and Hugh Budd bought him out. Forty-year-old William Hiram Morrison, a Columbia University graduate and Wall Street real estate attorney, then joined them under a new name of Morrison, Stapylton & Company. Together they ventured into the financial world when the firm opened a private or so-called "convenience" bank in a large general store with the only safe in Leesburg, Baer and Campbell. Located on the southeast corner of Fourth and Main, the bank opened April 1, 1886—the first bank established in Leesburg. Later they built the first brick building in town and relocated to the southwest corner of Sixth and Main.

Frank Cooke reported that 16% to 20% interest was charged on loans. Interest on invested deposits, he believed, was "only 8%."

In the meantime Stapylton's new partner,

MORRISON, STAPYLTON & CO.,
BANKERS,
LEESBURG, LAKE COUNTY, FLA.

A GENERAL BANKING BUSINESS CONDUCTED.
MORTGAGE LOANS
Negotiated on Bearing Groves and Improved Property.
REAL ESTATE DEPARTMENT.

Our system of avoiding the usual publicity of the Real Estate business, and of privately negotiating sales and purchases, gives us control of the choicest properties in the Lake Region. We make a specialty of sound investments in Wild Lands and Bearing Groves. Our responsibility assures to our customers good titles and good value. Correspondence solicited. New York Correspondents: Bank of Manhattan Co.

Morrison, who was not active in the bank's management, created some real estate ventures of his own.

March 26, 1886, or just before the bank opened, Morrison, for $269.25, rented hammock land on Lake Griffin from William H. McCormack of Leesburg, containing, with the exception of the lime trees, 2,054 "sweet seedling nursery orange trees, some of them budded." Under the one-year agreement Morrison, his agents or employees could enter the grove at reasonable times "to view the trees, dig, cultivate, bud or remove them." G. C. Stapylton witnessed the agreement. This transaction may have been for the benefit of the students and others who were trying to re-establish their groves after a hard freeze during the winter of 1886 or for planting on his Lake Ella property.

Then Morrison formed two companies—the Chetwynd Land Company and the Chetwynd Improvement Company—to develop communities on either side of *Stapylton's Sub-division* on Lake Ella which, as a town site, would become known as Chetwynd by June 1887.

The Town of Dundee and the Chetwynd Improvement Company

October 9, 1885, "Herndon's Plan of the Town of Dundee on the Florida Southern Railroad, 7 miles from Leesburg" had been filed in Sumter County. This town was to have been located in Section 28 directly east of the town of Chetwynd and across what is now US Route 441 and north towards Lady Lake.

The Florida Southern Railway dissected the proposed town that stopped at the Chetwynd station and post office twice a day for mail delivery. Colonist Philip F. Dietz ran a general store near the station. William T. Kennedy [*The History of Lake County,*

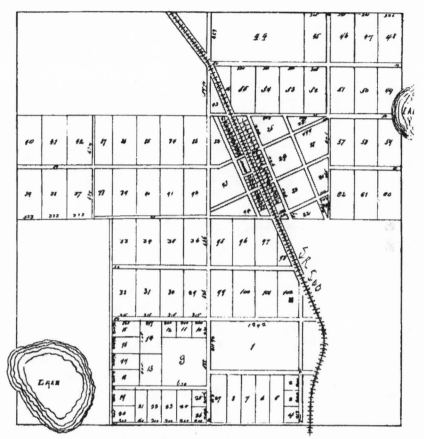

Plat Map of Dundee, October 9, 1885.

Florida, 1929] wrote, "There were seven or eight stores in the vale of Chetwynd Hill."

The Chetwynd Improvement Company incorporated in the State of Florida February 18, 1887. May 7, 1887, William H. and Helen B. Morrison sold 30 acres of land in the southeast quarter of Section 28 to The Chetwynd Improvement Company for $10,000. Witnesses to this transaction were G. C. Stapylton; Alex Cazalet, and M. B. Burr. Morrison had purchased this land

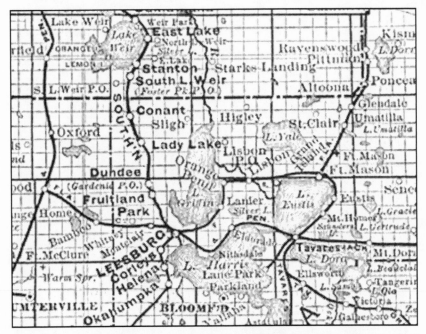

A sectional map of the eastern and southeastern portion of the state of
Florida, issued in 1888 by the land department of the Florida Southern
Railway Company. Dundee, rather than Chetwynd, was shown.

Florida Center for Instructional Technology, University of South Florida.

from Hugh Budd, a Stapylton and Company partner, and John
G. Herndon, an officer of the Sumter County Florida Land
Company.

In addition to the 30 acres sold, the deed's description of
the land adds "and also all of that part of the South East quarter
of the South quarter of the same Section Township and Range
aforesaid, which lies West of the Centre of the road bed of the
Florida Southern Railroad subject to the right of way of said
Railroad and containing about six acres [previously owned by
Budd] more or less." Budd retained ownership of 34 acres on
the east side of the Florida Southern railroad tracks.

One Dundee lot was sold to Alex Cazalet and another six

The Chetwynd Depot. Stores can be seen in the background.

lots to the Rev. William Cosens, father of colonists Sidney, Charles, and Francis, by the Chetwynd Improvement Company. No other transactions are listed for the company in the indexes of Sumter and Lake Counties until 1903, when the east half of the southeast quarter was sold to William Fussell & Company. The remainder, except for Lot 2 block 15 (Cazalet) and Lot 2 block 17 (unknown), was sold to John D. Robertson July 11, 1905, by the Chetwynd Improvement Company. All were subject to the right of way of the Florida Southern Railroad "as now used through or over the southwest quarter of the north quarter of Section 28."

Other Dundee land was purchased and retained by partners Thomas Herndon and Thaddeus Mosely. Herndon and Mosely sold a half interest in 19 Dundee lots in 1894 to colonist Frederick S. A. Maude. Land ownership either changed hands several times or the land was simply abandoned, according to tax lists.

The towns of Chetwynd and Dundee in Section 28 were not the only proposed developments near Lake Ella.

The Chetwynd Land Company

The Chetwynd Land Company, Sumter County, Florida, filed a platted map January 18, 1887. The area platted, including street names and a block designated for a hotel, covered all of Section 29 or the area directly west of Lake Ella that included 10 lots in a section originally platted for *Stapylton's Sub-division* in 1884. That land, previously owned by Stapylton, his father

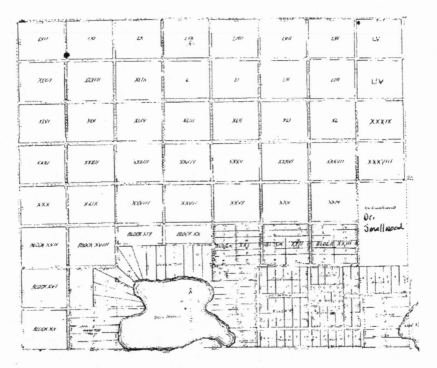

Plat Map of the Chetlynd Land Company, January 18, 1887.

William, as well as additional land owned by Stapylton's cousin, George Stapylton Barnes, was sold to William Morrison and Dr. Samuel Smallwood of Astoria, New York. It also included Deer Lake which, according to a satellite map, has completely disappeared.

A section of land, as in Section 29, comprises 640 acres. March 2, 1887, Morrison and Smallwood sold a fraction over 614 acres to The Chetwynd Land Company for $16,000 two months after the area was platted. The remaining acreage was retained by Smallwood, whose property was near Lake Ella in the southeast portion of that section. The Chetwynd Land Company then incorporated April 22, 1887.

Public records in Sumter County and Lake County show that, like Stapylton's subdivision of Chetwynd and Herndon's of Dundee, this venture never got off the ground. Only three sales were recorded in Sumter County; none in Lake County.

June 6, 1892, Leonard A. Bradley, a New York City real estate attorney bought, at a foreclosure sale, all of the land with the exception of Smallwood's acreage, for $1,500. The deed notes that Bradley was a trustee for William H. Morrison, Samuel B. Smallwood, William H. Prior and Charles S. Allen, as complainants against the Chetwynd Land Company, and the Chetwynd Improvement Company.

By 1893 The Central and Peninsular Railroad owned all but the northeast quarter of Section 29. That portion was owned by the Southern Florida Railway Company.

Morrison's real estate speculations in Lake County failed. In 1890 all of the assets of Morrison, Stapylton and Company were assigned to Stapylton when Morrison retired and moved to Warwick, Rhode Island.

The following year, 1891, "the beautiful" Maude Morrison,

referred to by Frank Cooke as "the belle of the colony" and coincidentally the daughter of Morrison and his wife, Helen Burr, married Frederick Chetwynd-Stapylton, a broker and a member of the London Stock Exchange—and Granville Chetwynd-Stapylton's older brother.

By 1904 the Morrison family was living in Lothburg, England, where William traded in American securities. That year he sold all of his remaining land in Lake County to John D. Robertson, of Ocala, the king of timber and turpentine.

Chapter Fifteen

Of Beans, Banks . . . and Kaolin?

STILL EAGER TO attract settlers to the area, the Lake County Immigration Association, G. C. Stapylton, treasurer, produced an information circular in 1888 extolling the benefits of living in Lake County. In addition to Stapylton and others representing the county's towns, G.H.A. Elin of Chetwynd and O. P. Rooks of Gardenia (Fruitland Park) were named as contacts for further information.

In spite of some failures, Stapylton's interest continued in the local real estate market. April 24, 1894, as secretary of the Leesburg Development Corporation (L. B. Lee, president), a plat of East Leesburg was laid out specifically for him. While the new corporation transacted seven sales, dozens of deeds are registered that Stapylton personally bought and sold in Leesburg. At his death Stapylton owned 260 shares and claims on 540 shares of the corporation.

Although a public record could not be found, Judge William Sherman Jennings of Brooksville, according to a letter Stapylton wrote him October 5, 1899, owned ten acres on the west side of Lake Griffin. Stapylton added that Stapylton and Company had a $200 purchase contract net of all but a ten percent commission. Whether the contract was honored is not known. What is known is that the following year Jennings, former head of the Democrat party, was elected Florida's governor.

Governor William Jennings

From March 7 to March 17 of 1902, Stapylton and Company, of all things, endeavored to sell 150 bushels of beans or almost a railroad carload for Jennings "at $.75 per hundred pounds which we make $.70 net to you. Could have done better before the thresher was moved away. Must now deliver at Fruitland Park, which however is nearer than Leesburg." The governor responded, "I am not sufficiently familiar with the weight of velvet beans in the hull to know what this will amount to per bushel or per barrell. I understand that a barrell in the hull is equivalent to a bushel with the hull off." Ultimately an old thresher was fired up and the whole crop of beans off the Picciola grove was shipped for $1.00 a bushel—shelled and hulls included, "making the price to you $.90."

The Leesburg and County State Bank

After Morrison's-departure, Morrison, Stapylton and Company was incorporated March 19, 1890, as the Leesburg and County State Bank—G. C. Stapylton, president, H. S. Budd, cashier and

G. CHETWYND STAPLETON, President,	H. S. BUDD, Cashier,	R. F. E. COOKE, Asst. Cashier.

The Leesburg & County
State Bank.

A General Banking business transacted. *Deposit Accounts* received on favorable terms. Foreign and Domestic *Exchange* bought and sold. Careful attention paid to *Collections* and proceeds remitted promptly. Money invested for customers on *First Mortgages* or other securities.

CORRESPONDENTS:—Bank of Manhattan Company, New York; Merchants National Bank, National Bank of the State of Florida, First National Bank of Florida, Jacksonville, Fla.; Melville, Fickus & Co., London, Eng.

The Leesburg and County State Bank, Leesburg, Florida.

R.F.E. Cooke, assistant cashier. "Stapylton is most enthusiastic," wrote Cooke.

A few months before Cooke had written his father George that he'd been offered a partnership for £4000 or the equivalent of $19,500. Cooke offered $5,000 less. The senior Cooke paid the price. Then the junior Cooke wrote back to request a box of Waverly pens. A dip pen from Waverly Pens of Edinburgh, Scotland, was one of the finest produced. Its smooth point prevented the paper from catching the nib—the pointed end that distributes the ink. A box sold for about $.75.

Duncan B. Campbell, a Scotch-Canadian and the co-owner of the general store with a safe, was named a director along with two men from the colony, Frederick S. A. Maude and Walter Neve. They owned and operated Maude and Neve, an up-scale livery stable in Leesburg..

Cooke complained about a new law the Florida legislature passed in 1891 that "we cannot loan money at more than 10% and pay full taxes on a sworn statement." He doubted that any banker would comply with the law.

With reference to his father's $2,500 deposit Cooke wrote, "It is against our rules to give interest on deposits. Consider investing it in, say, mortgages at 8% to 10%, or railroad bonds at 4 or 5%. I dare say we could manage it for you. The mortgages would be in a bearing grove or good city property."

Aside from real estate and banking, the phenomenon of electricity seems to have fascinated Stapylton. In 1891 he, along with W. D. Taylor and B. R. Milam, formed the Leesburg Electric Light and Water Power Company with a capitalization of $50,000. It wasn't until 1909, however, that J. Y. Clark was granted a franchise to start up electrical services for the town.

About 1891 the Leesburg Telephone Exchange strung wires from tree-to-tree along the town streets that enabled telephone calls within a radius of seven to ten miles. Efforts were also underway to connect Leesburg with New York (completed later in the year) and then with London. Stapylton had one of the few telephones in the area on his desk. As the story goes, when there was a fire someone called him at the bank. He then ran from his office on Main Street to Orange Street, about a block away, to ring the fire bell.

For Stapylton the year 1893 was stressful. The worst bank panic and economic depression in United States history blindsided the nation that March. But it didn't impact the Leesburg bank until the following July when the bank in Tavares, Lake County's seat, closed its doors. "We may have a run. We are, however, prepared, keeping cash in the vault," wrote Cooke. "Our fear is of being robbed, but we have hired a watchman for a steady patrol. At the present moment we have enough cash to pay a third of deposits, enough at our correspondent banks to pay another third, and we have good credit, so should be able to pay everything."

The Standard Kaolin Company

Shortly before the bank panic Stapylton, along with Samuel A. Teague of Lady Lake; W. A. Fulton; Alfred Allen, and F. A. Teague of Ocala; David and Mary Newcomb of Henderson County, Kentucky; James K. Whitaker of New York City, and Stapylton's partners, Hugh Budd and Frank Cook, filed a corporation charter with the Secretary of State under the name, Standard Kaolin Company, June 22, 1893. It wasn't recorded until September 3, 1895. With a capitalization of $600,000—most of that amount represented by the ownership of 3,500 acres in Lake County—this company sought to, among other purposes, mine kaolin and then manufacture it.

Kaolin, a soft white clay that is free of impurities such as iron, is an essential ingredient of porcelain used, for example, to make electrical insulators, china marbles, and ceramics. Fine china contains the very best grade of kaolin. Having been a geology student, it is not surprising that Stapylton, as the corporate treasurer, got involved in forming such a company. He owned a half-interest in 1,700 acres and one-third of the proceeds of 207 shares of the company.

In a September 6, 1893, letter to the Tariff Committee of the Congressional House Ways and Means Committee, Samuel Teague, Standard's president, wrote, "Within the last few years large deposits of the finest quality of kaolin or china clay have been discovered in Putnam and Lake Counties, Florida. Several plants have been erected for the preparation of the kaolin for market, and the business will soon grow into large proportions if present conditions remain and the present tariff of $3 per ton on foreign clays is not removed." He went on to write, ". . . that if the duty is removed we can not go into the market at all and that our already large investments in the clay beds are practically lost."

"Two plants are already in successful operation," Teague's letter continued. Although plant locations cannot be determined, they may have been along side the Palatlakaha River, a waterway that connects the lakes between Lake Harris in Leesburg to Lake Louise near Clermont. The Lake County Clay Company and the Florida China Clay Company both mined there.

By February 1895, Hugh Budd, according to Frank Cooke, urged Cooke's father "to redeem the mortgages on that kaolin land and let us invest the money in some other land." Until the company dissolved in 1936, public records only disclose dozens of Lake County land transactions.

Along with the burdens of a new business involvement and the anxiety of keeping his bank solvent, a great personal loss confronted Stapylton. His mother, Elizabeth, died September 18, 1893, in London. The Stapylton family immediately set sail for England.

The town site of Chetwynd had already folded and the colony's population dwindled. Finding the five-mile horseback commute from his home on Zephyr Lake to Leesburg inconvenient, Stapylton and his family moved to Leesburg in 1895 where they lived for awhile in St. James Episcopal Church's new rectory on Lee Street before moving to a home in the Gold Block, so named, it is reckoned, for a railroad contractor named Gold.

In all probability the relocation was prompted not only by the Depression that lasted until 1897 and his determination to keep the doors of the Leesburg and County State Bank open, but because of devastating freezes in late December 1894 and early February 1895, that completely destroyed and ended citrus production for years.

Chapter Sixteen

The Great Freeze

I N 1883 James William Gambier, the managing director of the Florida Land and Mortgage Company, a huge land company operative in 29 Florida counties, wrote in a prospectus, ". . . the latitude is far enough south to assure any serious injury [to citrus] from cold."

Although there had been two significant freezes during the previous decade, by 1890 the citrus industry was booming in Lake County. Money was being made on every side, and that money was being reinvested in new and larger groves. Growers glowingly predicted that the 1894 season would be a bumper crop year. By this time central Florida produced nearly all of the citrus grown in Florida with over three-quarters of the entire crop being shipped from Ocala, the seat of Marion County.

December 12, 1894, Frank Cooke wrote his father about the citrus he had recently sent to him: "Oranges sent off Stapylton & Co.'s groves; grapefruit and tangerines from my own place. I have about 25 boxes of grapefruit and 40 boxes of tangerines but selling them is such a lottery."

A little over two weeks later came the first round of the Great Freeze and in a single night Florida's entire citrus crop was reduced to pulp. The fruits of nearly every grove were destroyed; over four million boxes of luscious fruit were killed on the tree.

Christmas Day, 1894, it was reported that it was warm enough to swim. Over the next couple of days, however, it grew colder. Louis Bosanquet, like his brother, Augustus, before him, kept a record of dates that the temperature fell below 30 degrees. Reading from a thermometer located on the north side of the veranda of his home near Zephyr Lake, Bosanquet wrote, "December 28, 1894, 12 degrees, fruit frozen."

The Great Freeze destroyed ripened citrus, December 1894.

To his father Cooke wrote the next day,

We have just had a most disastrous frost—last night the thermometer went down to about 16 degrees and consequently all the unshipped orange crop, estimated at about 2-3/4 million boxes, has been *entirely* destroyed and the only question now is whether the trees are all hurt. The general opinion is that they are.

The outlook in this section is most serious. I suppose at least 75 percent of the crop in the neighborhood was being held for a better market and so are all destroyed & what we are all going to do until the next crop comes in a years time without any money I don't know. It seems to be perfectly useless to hope that the reports are exaggerated but I hope they may be. I never have seen a bluer or a sicker lot of people in my life though they take it pretty well considering and tell you with a chuckle that they have lost 10 or 12,000 boxes. One man was immensely delighted because he managed to sell his crop of 12,000 boxes for $50 or about $.004 a box. Guess we will pull through all right anyway.

Then the weather turned quite warm and after a good rain the trees shed their fruit and leaves. Little else of the trees were damaged. Within a few weeks the trees sprouted new growth. February 1, 1895, Cooke wrote, "The old trees are beginning to bud out again, but the young ones at best only show a flicker of life. It is rather annoying to hear you are still enjoying the oranges when we have absolutely none. By the papers they are actually importing them from the West Indies." Within a week after Cooke's writing the second round of the Great Freeze, this one of catastrophic consequences, blanketed the area.

"February 8, 1895: 12 degrees the Big Freeze," wrote Bosanquet. Having lost their foliage and being full of sap, the trees could not withstand another hard freeze. As the temperature plunged, the bark on the trees began to split, and the trees literally exploded, leaving the groves a grim and gruesome sight. Most of the trees were killed to the ground. The personal losses and the economic impact were enormous.

There was no money nor work nor much to eat. People survived on the likes of rabbits, turtles, and cabbage. Home and land values fell, while little business was transacted. Money deposited in banks was worth no more than fifteen cents on the dollar. People left in utter panic and despair or made plans to do so. Colony residents fled, leaving everything behind, including, as Louis Bosanquet's son Alfred recalled hearing, "the silver on the table." The Colony of Chetwynd became a ghost colony.

By 1900 only 15 Chetwynd gentlemen and their families—those with some financial resources and/or the ingenuity to diversify their crops or occupational interests—remained in Lake County.

Trees completely frozen, February 8, 1895.

Stapylton, the Receiver

"We have just had another bank flurry," Cooke wrote December 12, 1894, about two weeks before the freeze. "This time our esteemed competitor has not only distinguished but extinguished himself. His bank knows him no more. The excitement arose last Saturday when the Jacksonville papers arrived with an account of how he [Ernest Yager] had gone to the mint in New Orleans and said he had some gold bricks he wished to sell. On examination they proved to be brass. He had been 'buncoed' by confidence men [at a Palatka hotel] who made $6,000 out of him. It was lucky the news didn't reach town till after banking hours Saturday, else there would have been a run. I am sure the bank (his bank I mean, of course) could not have stood long."

The Bank of Leesburg began operations the same year as Morrison and Stapylton. Founded by Yager and his brother, Arthur, the bank found itself in dire straits to the point where an assignment needed to be made and to close the bank.

As Stapylton rode into town one morning, R. P. Burton, one of the bank's directors, stopped him to ask if he would accept the assignment. Stapylton responded, "Let me see Budd and if it is agreeable to him, I will. I will let you know in a few minutes." Stapylton and Budd agreed. February 12, 1895, the Bank of Leesburg, was assigned to Stapylton, because it was felt, according to the *New York Times*, that his bank could pay dollar for dollar.

In the wake of the freezes every bank between Jacksonville and Tampa suspended business but not the Leesburg County and State Bank—Stapylton's bank. Although deposits plunged from $175,000 to below $40,000 in four years, the bank's doors stayed open. But people's lives were ruined. "What are we going to do until the next crop comes . . . without any money?" wrote Frank Cooke to his father. "I never have seen a bluer or sicker lot of people," he reiterated.

Years later, a Lake County resident, Reuben D. Mathews, recalled an incident with Stapylton during this dark and dismal period. Mathews met with Stapylton and shared his business needs and worries with him. "But how will you live?" asked Stapylton. Young Mathews laughed but made no reply. Stapylton looked at him quizzically and remarked, "I see you can laugh. If you can laugh then you can live."

To the north in Marion County the last two Ocala banks in town suffered huge misfortunes. The First National Bank closed when its president was convicted of embezzling money from the Merchant's National Bank. When Federal agents arrived at his home one night to arrest him, he committed suicide in his upstairs bedroom. Already reeling in the financial aftermath of the Great Freeze which caught them holding mortgages on worthless land, Merchant's Bank also closed. The assets of both banks were assigned to a receiver, G. Chetwynd-Stapylton. His stature as a successful banker grew large.

State-wide, he served as the second vice president of the Florida Bankers Association. Speaking of bank failures at their 1896 convention in Jacksonville he said,

> It is difficult to exaggerate the moral and material injury that a community sustains by a bank failure. The worst side of human nature is unfailingly brought out and exhibits itself naked and unashamed. Loss of faith in mankind and in the stability of all human institutions follows a bank failure, and renders many of its victims, for a time at least, cynical, suspicious and unreasonable. The shock to public confidence does incalculable harm to the cause of banking.

While dealing with Ocala's financial disasters Stapylton lived there off and on for a couple of years or so where he sang in a church choir, presumably the Grace Episcopal Church Choir. Some years later a gentleman who sang with him wrote Stapylton's son, Brian, that his most vivid memory of Brian's father was the fascination of watching his Adam's apple move up and down when he was singing.

Chapter Seventeen

The Beginning of the End

I T WAS thought that a hard destructive freeze occurred no often than every 40 to 50 years in Florida. There had been, however, four major freezes since the British settled in Chetwynd. There was to be yet another. Perhaps colonist Frederick S. A. Maude had an inkling of an impending disaster.

December 2, 1898, Maude prepared his groves near West Apopka. He gathered a lot of wood, which was to be placed upon a number of fat light-wood knots between each tree. He planned to use turpentine chips along with a cheap grade of coal in order to start a quick fire with a lighted torch. A pile of sawdust nearby would be thrown on the fire to produce dense smoke. Nearby were barrels filled with water. Thermometers hung from trees throughout the grove. Maude had braced himself and his groves for the worst.

During the Valentine week of 1899, the Great Blizzard, one of the top-ten snow storms in the United States, hammered the South, including Florida. Sometimes called "Florida's Bluest Monday," February 13, 1899, rain turned to sleet and then to snow. The temperature in Chetwynd dipped to 15 degrees.

Wrote Louis Bosanquet, "Fruit frozen, trees killed, severe freeze; on the 15th snow on the veranda; one of the worst freezes on record." What few citrus trees remained after the Great Freeze four years before were completely destroyed—Fred Maude's probably along with them.

The 1899 freeze spelled the death knell.

Colonist George Winter had a slightly better fate. According to a family researcher, "A severe frost killed all the trees for miles around but when one of his trees survived, people from all parts of the country came to see 'Winter's Tree which could stand the frost.' The tree was still alive and bearing fruit in the 1950s, but it is not known whether other trees were propagated from it."

Coinciding with the fatal freeze was the official end of the Spanish-American War that began in 1898. Two colonists,

Charles Richard Bosanquet and Villiers Chernocke Smith, neither of them American citizens, served in Company B of the 1st Florida Volunteer Infantry Regiment. Although the unit never saw combat in Cuba, the company kept busy—marching and pitching tents.

COMPANY B 1ST FLORIDA VOLUNTEER INFANTRY
REGIMENT
This Company left Leesburg, Florida, on May 14th, 1898, by order of Adjutant General Houston, of the State of Florida, for Tampa, to be mustered into United States service. They arrived at Tampa on the same date and camped at Fort Brooke; mustered into United States service on May 20th, 1898. On May 27th they broke camp and marched a distance of two miles to DeSoto Park and pitched camp; left Desoto Park for Fernandina, Florida, by rail, on July 21st, 1898; arrived in Fernandina on July 22nd; marched one mile and pitched camp; left Fernandina, Florida on August 22nd, 1898, for Huntsville, Alabama; camped that night in the streets of Fernandina; left on August 23rd for Huntsville, arrived there on August 25th. Marched one and half miles and pitched a temporary camp in shelter tents; on August 26th marched one mile to the permanent camp. This Company transferred to the 3rd Battalion to be retained in the service on September 29th, 1898; mustered out of service on January 27th, 1899.

With the war over and perhaps envisioning new business opportunities in Cuba, Stapylton became involved in the establishment of a so-called "Ocala Colony" in Havana that by March 1901 comprised at least a dozen men and their families.

Sometime in January 1900 he and Elizabeth moved to Havana to "engage in business." J. O. LaFontisee, a reporter from the *Havana Post*, ". . . could not remember the nature of same, but is doing well, as he deserved." The *Ocala Evening Star* reported that Stapylton shared an office with Joe Woodrow who worked in the engineering department of the United States government. Family members surmise that Stapylton may also have been employed by the government. All that is known for

Prado, Havana, Cuba

certain is that he and Elizabeth lived in Cuba until April 1901. By then their two young children, Ella and Brian, were boarded at schools in England.

Nine months after moving to Havana, the couple contracted yellow fever and became seriously ill—Elizabeth more seriously than her husband. At that time yellow fever was the scourge of Cuba; loss of life from the disease exceeded those who died from military operations during the Spanish-American War. Procedures were put in place, not only to eradicate disease-carrying mosquitoes, but to have every new resident registered, not only at an immigration station but with a local hospital, presumably, in the case of the Stapyltons, a U.S. military hospital. Further, they were instructed to immediately notify authorities of the infection whereupon their home or apartment was to have been screened and a guard placed outside the door while the occupants were hospitalized.

Typically, the symptoms of the viral fever, especially the yellowing of the skin and eyes is followed by a short period of remission; which usually leads to recovery. According to the Stapylton's friend, Frederick Schreiber, as reported in the September 14, 1900, edition of the *Ocala Evening Star*, both were convalescing and out of danger. They left Havana in April 1901 and returned to their "Gold Block" home in Leesburg.

By this time Leesburg's population had risen to 722 residents. Stapylton's political star also rose—both state-wide and locally. It seemed inevitable that, "G. C. Stapylton, so well and so favorably known here as the receiver of our defunct banks several years ago, was nominated by the democracy of Leesburg as its next mayor [and magistrate, a dual office]. He will make a splendid official," the *Ocala Evening Star* reported January 6, 1902. The following month he was elected. At his first court as magistrate he fined two prominent citizens for indulging in a scrapping match. "We of Ocala know his honor, Mayor Stapylton, and feel confident he will reflect honor on the office he now occupies," the *Ocala Evening Star* boasted.

But Stapylton was not a healthy man. Not fully recovered from his bout with yellow fever, he learned that he had been infected with consumption (tuberculosis)—a disease that usually affects the lungs. He and his wife decided to go to England for rest and recuperation. Stapylton did not recover.

October 29, 1902, "A cable message to the Leesburg and County State Bank of Leesburg announced the death of the bank's president, G. Chetwynd-Stapylton, which occurred at his old home in London, England, Wednesday afternoon. He was a polished gentleman and a fine businessman." [*Ocala Evening Star*, October 31, 1902.]

Granville Brian Chetwynd-Stapylton, age 44, died, not "at his old home," but at the St. Michael and All Angels Rectory,

Hallaton, Leicestershire, England, where his father then served. Three days later his widow, Elizabeth, wrote Hugh Budd, one of his bank partners:

Hallaton Rectory
Uppingham
England
Nov. 3, 1902

Dear Mr. Budd,

My dear Granville was laid to rest here on Saturday—the 1st (All Saints Day). He had been in bed seven weeks but I am thankful to say that until the last two or three weeks he had been free from pain. Towards the end his throat became very painful but he bore that so patiently and as uncomplainingly as he had borne all the months of ill health and weakness that had preceded it. His end was so peaceful, much like a child sinking to sleep, truly a beautiful close to such a life as his has been. He had been praying and longing to be relieved. It has been such a comfort to have had him here with his father and all he loved. I know that everything was done for him that could be done. There have been many anxious weeks but rest has come for him at last.

With kind regards to you and Mr. Cooke and love to Mrs. Budd.

Yours very truly,

E. Chetwynd-Stapylton

October 11, 1887, Stapylton had signed a very simple will in the presence of his brother-in-law, Gustav Schneider, who had married Harriet Routledge; his Haileybury classmate and friend, Gerald Meysey Fellows, and his then business partner, Hugh S. Budd. After all debts were paid his entire estate was bequeathed to his wife, Elizabeth. It also named his executors: Budd and James Routledge, his wife's brother. Court appointed appraisers, Arthur L. Miller and R. Francis E. Cooke, valued Stapylton's estate at $2,139.55, including a gun valued at $7.50 and cash in the bank of $48.85. The estate, according to the probate file, was never closed.

His wife, Elizabeth, and their two children, Brian and Ella, remained in England where Elizabeth died June 29, 1943. It took about 25 years to dispose of all of the properties she and her husband owned. But nothing sold at a great price. Lots 21, 22, 23, 35 on Lake Ella, formerly known as Stapylton's Subdivision (Town of Chetwynd), sold for a grand total of $50.00 in 1905.

January 26, 1949, Lady Ella Gillette and Brian Stapylton sold the last parcel of their father's land, located in the *Home Estate,* to Margaret Cooke, the widow of Frank Cooke.

Two decades after Stapylton's death the *Leesburg Commercial* wrote of him: "In the early days this doughty Englishman put his money into the bank that was destined to live and thrive and prosper long years after he tired of 'pioneering' and returned to his home in England. He had the characteristics that in those days were popularly attributed to bankers, being aloof and formal in business hours, but he was staunch in his friendships and the soul of his honor."

Stapylton Remembered

American football, derived from English rugby football, got its start in 1872. A fierce rivalry grew between Harvard and Yale that continues to this day. The November 29, 1894, issue of *The Nation* reported on what is currently known as the most brutal football game ever witnessed in the United States. Seven of the 22 starters were severely injured—all of them intentionally. The writer compared the game to a Roman arena. The game was so violent that the series was suspended for two years following. Stapylton, obviously, had access to the magazine that focuses on politics and culture and responded to the article. His letter iterates some of the experiences of Stapylton's personal game of life:

To the Editor of the Nation

Sir:

In your article on "The New Football" you say that, if the game now played be a useful preparation for modern life, then all students ought to be compelled to play it. Twenty years ago it was the practice at several of the large public schools in England to compel all students to play, and I presume the usage still remains. At Haileybury College, where I was a student, compulsory football twice a week during the winter term was a regulation from which no boy was allowed to escape unless pronounced unfit by the college physician. I believe that this feature of school life was certainly advantageous in developing in the boys the manly qualities of activity, hardihood, and courage. A lack of pluck on the football field was something that no boy dared to show, whatever his natural timidity. While occasionally accidents would happen, they were very rarely serious, and they were invariably accidents. I think that this statement would be true today as applied to football in England when played by the upper and middle classes. In my time, at all events, any player who was believed to be guilty of intentionally injuring another would have met with the contempt and disgust of his associates, and would have been driven from the field in future by the social ostracism that would have followed his misdeed. But such conduct was practically never heard of. It was rendered impossible by a pervading spirit of fair play and of right, gentlemanly, and sportsmanlike behavior at all games. Without this guiding and restraining sentiment no game can flourish, and, until it can be infused into the minds of present-day collegians, they will continue to degrade the game into an exhibition of brutal ruffianism.

Part Two

The Chetwynd Colonists
1882–1902

Over the chronicled twenty years or so, Chetwynd not only vanished but so did most of the people who chose to settle in the colony. Whatever their hopes and dreams had been, Chetwynd was probably recalled as a notable but brief stopover along their way to somewhere. Who were they? Where did they go? What did they do with the rest of their lives?

WHILE NO doubt incomplete, this digest of biographical sketches of (British) Chetwynd colonists was compiled from various sources—the 1885 Florida Census, Sumter County; United States and English censuses; the earliest Holy Trinity Episcopal Church parish records, as well as those of St. James Episcopal Church, Leesburg; recorded deeds of Sumter and Lake Counties, Florida; an 1886 letter to the *New York Herald,* and the membership lists of the Bucket and Dipper Club, a social club in the colony. Additional sources for information, where provided, were gleaned from online genealogical and historical resources, local histories, and newspaper items.

Nearly all of the surnames were originally preceded by initials only—most times three of them—which made confirming identities for biographical information challenging. A note of caution: a few of those listed may not have lived in the colony. They may have been British investors only.

Keep in mind also that not all of those listed resided in the colony at the same time nor did they arrive in the colony at the same time. Factual evidence based upon deeds, Bucket and Dipper Club membership records and ship manifests shows that 28 people lived in the colony prior to the June 30, 1885 Florida Census. That census identified forty people of British birth in District 1—the district that included the northwest portion of present Lake County. Of that number 28 were single men, two single women, four couples, and two young children. Twenty-two of the 32 men were under thirty-years old. Only one listed his occupation as an orange grower.

Bucket and Dipper Club membership lists also provide a clue that most averaged a residency of four to five years. A dozen men and their families and three unmarried women remained in Lake County until death—Louis Bosanquet; Hugh Budd; Charles Chesshyre; R.F.E. (Frank) Cooke; George Coulson; Earle Geary; Joseph Hannah; Louis Kenny; Stephen Reynolds; Villiers Smith; John Vickers-Smith and his sisters, Sarah, Margaret, and Elizabeth, and George Winter.

Although most of the young men probably received some sort of monetary allowances from home, these young pioneers, as a whole, were not disinherited or black-sheep remittance men who were sent away and paid to stay away, as claimed in previous historical or fictional accounts. They were, for the most part, well-educated sons of English ladies and gentlemen in no particular birth order.

Allenson, W. T. was a signer of the letter to the *New York Herald* in 1886, and owned about five acres near Stapylton and Company on Zephyr Lake.

Back, William Henry, a solicitor, was born July 20, 1853, in Ewell, Surry, England. He married Marion Edith Brown in 1885, and had ten children. They owned 160 acres, probably as investors only, that were sold to G. C. Staplyton for £1($4.86) in 1899.

Back, George Reid, born October 25, 1854, Ewell, Surry, he came to this country May 10, 1884, aboard the *Adriatic*. He left the colony by April 1888, and set out for Boston, where he married Josephine McChenney June 2, 1891. Shortly thereafter, the couple moved to Gothenburg, Nebraska. There they raised two daughters, Josephine and Winifred, and a son, George Jr. George Sr. was naturalized in 1907. He owned and operated George Back, Lumber, Coal and Grain Company in Gothenburg and died there in 1939.

Back, Arthur Charles Lempriere, a mechanical engineer, was born May 27, 1864, in Hethersett, Norfolk, England. Although he owned land in the vicinity of Zephyr Lake, he also bought a lot in Leesburg from Josiah Lee. By 1891, however, he was living with his widowed mother at Hethersett Hall. Arthur died May 14, 1923, in Plymouth, England. He was survived by his wife, Mary Amelia Elderton, whom he married in 1901.

Arthur held Patent No. 26,2 A.D.1903, for Belt or Band Gearing:

> Arthur Charles, Lempriere Back. 14 Brandrette Road, Plymouth in the County of Devon. Engineer, do hereby declare the nature of this invention to be as follows: This invention relates to apparatus for the transmission of power. Its object being the construction of a pair of fast and loose grooved pulleys and striker pulleys upon which a band is run for the transmission of power . . .

Back, Percy James, born January 23, 1866, in Hethersett, Norfolk, England, purchased about 10 acres from Stapylton in April 1884. He apparently returned home soon after that; he died there August 22, 1885.

The parents of the four brothers, among 12 children, were Henry and Fanny Lempriere Back, landed gentry of England.

Barclay, Edmund Hay, a landowner in various parts of Lake County, was born November 26, 1859, in Arngask, Fifeshire, Scotland. By the 1900 U.S. Census he was enumerated as a farmer in Lane Park near Apopka, Florida, and by 1910 was an orange grower in Stanton, Florida. A University of St. Andrew's, Scotland, graduate, he died November 11, 1935, in Scotland.

Barclay, Walter Reginald Hay, was born May 20, 1861, in Arngask. By the 1900 U.S. Census he lived in Plant City, Florida, where he was a day laborer. He emigrated in 1883.

Barclay, William Herbert Hay, a librarian, was born May 21, 1861, also in Arngask. Never married, he died July 16, 1938, in Ft. Myers, Florida.

These three brothers were the sons of Jane Wilson and Arthur Hay Barclay, a "landed proprietor."

Barrett, F. A.

Barron, M. E. T.

Barrow, William Temple, born 1847, Surrey, England, died by March 15, 1886.

Bird, Robert and Annie Palmer's marriage, September 28, 1889, was the first recorded at Holy Trinity Church. Joseph Julian officiated. Both lived in Lady Lake, Florida, at the time but moved to England shortly thereafter.

Bleakley, W. H. died in the colony, but the date is not known.

Bonnett, Cyril Stephen was born in May 1, 1867, in Swarraton, Hampshire, England, the son of Alice and Stephen Bonnett, rector of Popham and Woodmancot. A colonist by 1885, he returned to Hampshire County by 1891, where he lived in Woodleigh Fleet. By 1917, Cyril was a London solicitor. He died in 1941.

Bosenquet, Augustus Percival, born October 26, 1860, in East Barnet, Hertfordshire, England, emigrated to Florida with his

**Augustus Percival
Bosanquet**

brother Eugene in 1882. The eldest Bosanquet son, Augustus was a rifleman with the Middlesex Militia before entering the Jesus College of Cambridge University, where he played rugby and studied languages. He continued his study of languages for two years in Wurttenberg, Germany, and then in Tours, France.

Augustus bought 100 acres near Zephyr Lake, from one of the Tanner brothers, Martin, and constructed a two-story, eleven-room mansion now called *Fair Oaks*. Augustus and Eugene also set out 20 acres of oranges along with their specialty, mandarins, and raised many other plants with seeds they brought with them from England. Among them was the Red Ceylon peach, the most tropical peach grown in Florida. A Holy Trinity founder, he left the United States in the early 1890s to become the secretary of the Royal British Club in Lisbon, Portugal. Never married, Augustus died

Fair Oaks

in Portugal May 11, 1930. The beneficiary of his estate was his nephew, Alfred, the son of Louis Bosanquet.

Bosanquet, Eugene Percival was born October 13, 1862, in Rochester, Kent, England. In 1886, he purchased a half-acre of land near his brother from Sam Tanner for $30 before going to work at the Alcaxa Hotel in Daytona, Florida. Tragically, Eugene was struck by a rattlesnake on the inside of his left leg above the ankle while hunting near Daytona with his friend Mr. Evelyn Walker. Walker tended to him, hoisted him up on his shoulders and carried him to Daytona where he died early February 2, 1892. He is buried at the Pinewood Cemetery in Daytona Beach.

Bosanquet, Louis Percival, Bosanquet son number three, was born July 20, 1865, and educated at Eton College in Buckingham, England. He arrived in Central Florida in 1888, to join his elder brothers. Louis married Ellen Lewis Hall of Marietta, Ohio, the daughter of John and Frances Ellen Hereford Hall, November 4, 1891, at her mother's home in Fruitland Park. A story goes that Ellen rode her horse to the Bosanquet Place in the early morning hours to flirt with Louis as he looked out an upstairs window in his nightshirt. An-

**Louis Percival
Bosanquet**

other version, according to Louis' grandson, Louis, is that Ellen was standing outside (on a porch) at her house and waved to Louis as he rode his horse one morning near the porch. "The argument my sisters had was Ellen in her nightgown or fully dressed?" Their marriage is said to have been scandalous. Ellen was a direct descendant of Betty Washington Hall, the sister of George Washington who stole the United States from Great Britain.

Louis and Ellen had three children, Frances, Louise and Alfred. Louis died April 30, 1930, and is buried at Holy Trinity, along with his wife, also called Nell, who died a year later, "not caring to live alone."

A horticulturalist extraordinaire, in the 1920s Louis grew, among other shrubs and plants, 14 varieties of bamboo; at least 14 varieties of palms; 100 varieties of fancy-leaf caladium; 75 varieties of roses; 16 varieties of crinum lilies along with citrons, which bore a heavy crop annually.

In the late 1920s Louis completely remodeled *Fair Oaks* and added a study to hold what is said to have been the largest collection of horticultural books in the State of Florida. Sold over a decade ago and presently unoccupied, *Fair Oaks* has gone from spectacular beauty to an ugly landscape of weeds and spindly trees.

Augustus, Eugene and Louis were the first three of six sons of Percival and Charlotte Bevan Bosanquet. For centuries Bosanquet families, descendants of French Huguenots, were well known as merchants and bankers in Great Britain.

Bosanquet, Charles Richard, born in April 21, 1865, Kent, England, to the Rev. Charles and Amelia Bosanquet, was a cousin of the Bosanquet brothers. When Charles arrived he farmed in Montclair and later bought a lot in Leesburg. He was a lay reader at St. John the Baptist Episcopal Church, Montclair, located about two miles west of Leesburg. During the Spanish-American War, Charles served as a private in the Leesburg Rifles, a unit that never left Florida, from June 28, 1898 to January 21, 1899. Charles returned to England shortly thereafter, lived in Tonbridge Falls, Kent, "on his own means," and died there in November of 1940.

Boswell, C. S.

Bovill, Owen Vallance, born in 1861, Laughton, Essex, England, was the son of Mary Owen and James Bovill, a corn factor—a middle man in corn dealing. Owen was a colony landowner by 1886. He moved on to Victoria, British Columbia, where he married Minna and established himself as a fruit grower and rancher. Owen died in London in 1934. He was one of five colonists who eventually went to live at the Coldstream Ranch, in Vernon, British Columbia.

Buckle, Claude William, born in 1869 in Aldingbourn Sussex, England. Claude arrived in the United States October 19, 1885, aboard the *Britanic*. He apparently had visited his family, Christopher and Caroline Buckle, in England the following

March. Fellow colonist, Gerald M. Fellows, accompanied Buckle on his return trip back to Florida. A civil engineer, Claude died February 15,1904, at Grosvenor House, Southampton.

Budd, Hugh Sandeman, born April 28, 1856, London, Middlesex, was the son of Edward and Antoinette Budd. After graduating from Trinity College, Cambridge, Hugh read law at

Left to right: Frank Cooke, Hugh Budd, and Frederick Maude.

Lincoln Inn, London, before coming to the colony for a visit in 1884. Hugh decided to stay. He was one of the three original partners of Staplyton & Company in 1885, a director of the Standard Kaolin Company, established in 1893, and was the executor of G. C. Stapylton's will. After Stapylton's death the Leesburg and County State Bank was voluntarily liquidated and July 22, 1903, became a private bank, Budd and Cooke. It was Budd who had the audacity to write Governor William Jennings that he had overdrawn his account by $54.90 later in 1903.

Frank Cooke wrote two anecdotes about Budd. Riding home one night, Budd ran over a skunk that roused everyone out of bed. Another night Budd's horse was nearly decapitated. It seems that someone erected a barbed-wire fence between the time Budd left for Leesburg and returned late at night. Budd was thrown from the horse but not hurt. There was no mention as to the fate of the horse.

September 5, 1894, Hugh married Gertrude Alden Hubbard, the daughter of David Lyman and Almeda Hubbard of Corley's Island, located south of Leesburg. They had two daughters: Hilda, born in August 1895, and Mary, born about 1901. At that time he was the president of the Leesburg Development Company. In the 1910 Lake County Census his occupation was listed as a "real estate manipulator." A Holy Trinity founder, by 1898 the Budd family had affiliated with St. James, Leesburg. Hugh died August 10, 1919, in Leesburg and is buried at Lone Oak Cemetery. According to the St. James parish register, he died "of a nervous breakdown." At his death Budd owned hundreds of acreage in the area.

Bush, George, born about 1867, was a bookkeeper who arrived in the colony about 1885 and boarded with the Josiah E. Lee family.

Cadell, James Ludovic, born March 21, 1872, in Edinburgh, Scotland, he emigrated to the United States in 1889. The Rt. Rev. William Crane Gray officiated at the marriage of James and Celia Dunn July 15, 1895, at Holy Trinity, Chetwynd. Their son, Robert Ludovic, was baptized October 3, 1897, also at Holy Trinity. By 1900 they were living in Citrus County, Florida. A few years later they moved to Vernon, British Columbia, and then to Tazmania where James died in 1914.

Cadell, Harry Nash, born August 13, 1879, in Bengal, India, returned to England by 1891. In September 1908, he, a rancher, and Eva Noble, his wife, came to the U.S. to visit his sister and brother-in-law, Elenora and John Vickers-Smith, in Fruitland Park. By 1910 they were living in Oregon City, Oregon, where Harry was engaged in real estate. He and Eva had at least three children: Harold, Margaret and Catherine. Harry died in 1940.

Elenora, James and Harry were children of Col. Robert and Geogina McKay Cadell of Cheltenham, Gloucester, England.

Cazalet, Alexander Paul Lewis, born September 9, 1844, St. Petersburg, Russia, the son of Louis and Nathalie (deHeering) Cazelet, arrived in the United States aboard the *Wyoming* February 18, 1885. Alex was the first secretary of Holy Trinity's Vestry. He was appointed a church warden at Holy Trinity in 1891 but left a few years later for Kynnersly, South Rhodesia (now Zimbabwe), where he became a captain of the British South African Mounted Police. He married Mary Eileen Bagnall and had three children: Natalie, Harold and Philip. Alex died January 31,1928.

Cazalet, Albert Edward, Alex's half-brother and referenced on some lists as "B.," was born August 16, 1867, also in St. Petersburg. B. lived in the colony by 1886. By 1890 he lived in Foldestone, England. But by 1911 he had moved to Vernon, British Columbia, where he died February 27, 1914. He was the son of Sarah Jane Mirrielees and Louis Cazalet.

Chetwynd-Stapleton, Granville Brian and **Ella Mabel** (see Part One). Granville and Elizabeth Chetwynd-Stapylton had two children, Granville Brian and Ella Mabel, who were both born in Chetwynd, Florida.

Granville Brian, named for his father, was born September 19, 1887. In 1895, at age eight, he left Florida for schooling, first at his father's alma mater, Haileybury, and then at the historic Charterhouse in Goldalming.

Granville Brian
Chetwynd-Stapylton

June 23, 1906, Brian, as he was called, was commissioned in 2nd Volunteer Battalion, The East Surrey Regiment, renamed in 1908 as the 5th Battalion. He served tours of duty with various units in India, the North West Frontier, Tigris, and South Kurdistan. After the 1914–18 War he rejoined the 5th Battalion and commanded it from 1924 to 1930. He was promoted to Brevet Colonel in 1927 and served with TARO from 1930 to 1936. From 1939 to 1943 he was County Army Welfare Officer and from 1943 to 1945 Command Army Welfare Officer, Southern Command. January 27, 1947, he was appointed Honorary Colonel of 381 (East Surrey) Anti-Tank Regiment RA (TA). Following military service he was a broker on the London Stock Exchange, the High Sheriff of Surrey in 1952, and warden of Whilsley Villages, Walton-on-Thames.

Brian married Catherine Lyne January 14, 1922, and had three daughters, Lucy, Mary Elizabeth, and Bridget. He died January 20, 1964.

Lady Ella Mabel was born November 22 1889 and educated in England. In 1911 she married Col. Sir William Alan Gillett. They had seven children: Elizabeth, Arthur, Granville, David, William, John and Stella.

Lady Ella Mabel Gillett

A Justice of the Peace, Lady Ella died June 11, 1974.

Chesshyre, Charles John Newton was born July 23,1860, the only son of barrister Charles John and Mary Susan Chesshyre of Cheltenham, Gloucestershire, England. Charles married Sarah Cressee Winter November 21, 1896, at St. John the Baptist Episcopal Church, Montclair, about eight years after he arrived in the colony. An attorney, Charles and Sarah, the sister of colonist George E. Winter, had five children: Ida, Alfred, Julia, Gertrude, and Charles William. The Chesshyres moved from the Zephyr Lake area to Leesburg shortly after the turn of the century. Charles died May 10, 1925, and is buried at Lone Oak Cemetery, Leesburg, with his wife and some of his children.

Collins, J. S.

Cooke, Robert Francis (Frank) Edward was born May 8, 1863, in Kensington, Norwich, England, the only son of George Frederick and Elizabeth Anne Payne Cooke. Frank had a younger sister, Jenette. A Cambridge rower (bow) and graduate, he emigrated May 9, 1886. Shortly after his arrival he snapped his first "instantaneous" picture and is probably responsible for many of the pictures in this book. An amateur photographer, Frank's dream was to buy-out a photography business in Leesburg to keep him going "until our groves begin to pay" but his father nixed that notion.

Frank is remembered locally as a prominent banker. In 1890 he joined G. C. Stapylton and Hugh Budd in a partnership at the Leesburg and County State Bank as the cashier. After Stapylton's death Hugh and Frank formed a partnership, bought out the other stockholders, and carried on the business under the name of Budd and Cooke, Bankers.

They dissolved their partnership in 1907 and applied for a new charter as the Leesburg State Bank; Hugh Budd, president,

M. P. Mickler, vice-president, and Frank Cooke, cashier. Hugh resigned shortly thereafter. Former Governor William S. Jennings was then elected president. Frank replaced Jennings in 1917 .

In 1925 the bank's directors decided to build a four story bank building across 6th Street from the original bank building, which was the largest office building in Lake County at that time. Ma Barker, the famous Depression-era bank robber, spent some time casing the Leesburg State Bank in 1930. She decided not to rob it, because security was too tight.

During the Great Depression the bank went into receivership after the bank moratorium in 1933 and never reopened. The First National Bank took over the bank and named Frank chairman of the board—a position he held until his death.

Among Frank's many other achievements he, in partnership with O. L. Fussell, built the first public packing house in Leesburg for washing, sizing and polishing citrus. After Fussell's death Frank maintained the business until 1928 when he sold out.

Frank and Ada at Niagara Falls.

A founder and member of Holy Trinity and many local civic organizations, it is written that Frank believed his biggest contribution to public life was the Thursday half-holiday. Leesburg merchants closed their businesses every Thursday afternoon during the summer months. This practice grew in popularity and by 1929, was statewide.

Frank married twice. October 9, 1906, he married Ada Gibb, daughter of Samuel Gibb of London, England, and the niece of Harriet Deal, at St. Stephen's Episcopal Church, Jacksonville, Florida. Clarence Frankel, a missionary priest who had served Holy Trinity a short time before, officiated. Frank's former roommate, Girard E. Murial, witnessed the marriage. Ada and Frank lived near Zephyr Lake and were neighbors of Charles Chesshyre and his family.

Ada, born December 7, 1881, in England, died March 19 1911, and is buried at Shiloh Cemetery in Fruitland Park. Obviously grief-stricken, Frank had the following inscribed on her tombstone, *The Hours I Spent with thee dear heart are like a string of pearls to me. I count them every one apart, my rosary, my rosary.*

April 5 1923, Frank married Margaret Grace Cameron, daughter of P. S. Hopkins of St. Louis, Missouri, and the widow of D. F. Cameron, in Leesburg. Villiers Chernocke Smith was a witness. Margaret was born May 11, 1885, in Missouri. Before their marriage she was a founder of St. Paul's Roman Catholic Church, established in Fruitland Park in 1921.

Frank had earlier acquired the site of Granville Stapylton's first home on Zephyr Lake, where he built a new home, *Franmar,* in 1924 for his new bride.

A polished, gentle, and erudite gentleman, Frank drove to Leesburg everyday in a light buggy with a high-stepping horse. Then he put the buggy aside and drove the first of two cars in Leesburg—a two-cylinder Cadillac.

After suffering several heart attacks, Frank died suddenly March 18, 1934. He was buried at Shiloh Cemetery next to his first wife, Ada, but was later exhumed and buried at the Hillcrest

Franmar

Memorial Gardens, Leesburg, alongside his second wife, Margaret, who died November 4, 1980. Gilbert Leach, editor of *The Commercial* and a good friend, wrote:

> How Frank Cooke ever found time to look after the details of all other folks' troubles he assumed, nobody has ever discovered. Widows came to him with their affairs and he did his best—which was good—to help them. Men of affairs sought his advice and assistance—and got both. Minor children who constituted an estate looked upon him as a godfather, and he did not fail them.

Cooper, Reginald H. T., a rowing competitor of Frank Cooke in England, was born September 30, 1866, in Rippingale, Lincolnshire, the son of the Rev. William and Catherine Miller Cooper, and emigrated to the U.S. in 1886. Two years later he sold his land to colonist J. H. B. Harrington and moved to Palatka, Florida.

September 2, 1891, he married Helen Geary, at St. James, Leesburg. For a short time Reginald and Helen, with their son, John, lived in Fayetteville, Tennessee, before returning to Palatka where Reginald was the secretary-treasurer of G. M Davis &

Son, manufacturers of cypress tanks. He died May 4, 1925, in Palatka. His wife, Helen, was a sister of colonist Earl Geary and of Emily Geary, who married Herbert Smith, also a colonist.

Cosens, Charles Hyde Champion, born in April 1863, lived in the colony a very short time. By 1900, he had married Florence Hicks in England and had two daughters, Dorothy and Elsie. Charles became a surgeon.

Cosens, Francis Robert Seppings, born about 1864, lived in the colony by 1886 and returned to England by 1891. Francis enlisted in the 1st Volunteer Battalion of the Leicestershire Regiment, and graduated from medical school in 1894, the same year he married Ettie Howat. By 1917 he was a Major in the Royal Army Medical Service. Frances and Ettie had a daughter, Marjorie, and a son, F. R. S. Cosens. who eventually commanded the 10th Gurka Rifles in India. Francis served on the committee to establish Holy Trinity.

Cosens, Sydney D. T., born about 1865, purchased property in Leesburg in 1885. By 1891 when he sold all of his properties he was living in Osceola County, Florida. In the June 1903 term of the Florida Supreme Court Sydney lost a suit for negligence by the Savannah, Florida and Western Railroad Co. A freight hauler at the Kissimmee depot, a train making track changes had killed his horse and "injured" his wagon and harness.

The Cosens brothers were the sons of Helen and William Cosens, Vicar of Dudley, England. They were born in Worcestershire, Middlesex, England, and came to the United States November 29, 1884, aboard the steamer Egypt. *Their father William bought Lot 12 in the town of Chetwynd for $101.60—the first lot sold in the subdivision.*

Coulson, George Francis was born October 20, 1845, to George Francis and Janet Isabelle Laurie Coulson of Glasgow, Scotland. Previously a clerk in Lancashire, England, George emigrated here in 1886. January 18, 1898, he married Madeleine DeFraine Harvey, wife of colonist Edwin J. Harvey, who left the area without his family. The Coulson's were enumerated in the 1900 Lady Lake (U.S.) census with her six children and their son, George Francis Laurie Coulson, who was baptized at Holy Trinity December 10, 1897. Another son, Ian Laurie, was born May 29, 1905, or shortly before his father died in 1908. George is buried at Lone Oak Cemetery, Leesburg. Madeleine (1869–1945) and her family continued to live in Lady Lake before moving to Leesburg about 1920.

Coulson, H. N. This gentleman is thought to have been Hugh Niven Coulson, the nephew of the above George Coulson. Hugh was born January 3, 1872, in Edinburgh, Scotland to John Laurie and Mary Niven Coulson. He died in 1901 in Devon, Somerset, England.

Cowen, George, born in May 1868, in Cumbria, Cumberland, England, with his brother, Robert, came to Central Florida by 1886.

Cowen, Robert Watson was the baptismal sponsor for the son of colonist George Francis Coulson. Born in May 1869 in Cumbria, Cumberland, England, Robert owned land on Lake Unity, Picciola, in Lake County. He left the colony in 1895. By the following year he was living in Fremantle, Colony of Western Australia, with his wife, Emily. Robert and George's sister, Marion, married colonist William Tennant Trimble in England.

George and Robert were sons of Robert Watson Cowen, owner of a cotton spinning company, and Henrietta Oliphant Cowen.

Creery, Alexander, born in March 1863, West Ashford, Kent, England, emigrated to the United States by June 1885. A classmate of G. C. Stapylton's at Haileybury College, Alex was the son of a solicitor, Leslie Creery, and his wife, Emily. In 1890 Alexander sold the land he'd purchased in 1889 for $1 to his mother for $3,000.

The Leading Race.
Left to right: Alexander Creery, Frederick Maude (winner), Henry Elin, George Elin, and Cyril Herford.

Dawn, Harold Frederick Leigh was Frank Cooke's roommate in Stapylton & Company's boarding house on Lake Zephyr in 1886. Born July 28, 1868, at Burgh Castle, Yarmouth, Norfolk, England, he was a son of William James and Cecilia Blane Dawn. Harold returned to England, where he married Adeline Marie Kerby December 6, 1901. The couple moved to Rangoon, India, where Harold was a rice broker. There he died January 25, 1911.

Dawson, George Seymour was born January 24, 1862, Midlothian, Scotland, to Col. Erskine S.F G. and Blanche Seymour Dawson. George was enumerated in the 1885 U.S. Census with

Augustus and Eugene Bosanquet as a jobber—one who works by the piece or at odd jobs. Dawson died November 20, 1888, at age 27, according to the parish register of St. James Episcopal Church, Leesburg.

Dietz, Phillip Fraser Digby, born June 1, 1862, in Marlebone, Middlesex, England, was a London clerk. A colony resident by 1886, Phillip managed the general store in Dundee before he returned to England in 1893. The son of a merchant trader Bernard and Melvilla Dietz, Phillip was elected a member of the Royal Geographical Society, London, in 1905.

Doudney, Alfred Cecil, born in Carlisle, Cumberland, England, September 24, 1866, arrived in the colony October 14, 1887. Two years later he moved to Sanford, Florida. There Alfred married Eliza Clarke Downing February 5, 1892, when he was very ill with typhoid fever. He was musically inclined and took part in many local and church "entertainments" in Sanford. He died there September 5, 1901.

Doudney, Raymond Pelly, baptized August 4, 1869, came to Florida September 8, 1892. By 1901 he was a second lieutenant in Ceylon and eight years later was working at the Western Motor Company in Bath, Somerset, England. A motor engineer Raymond invented "new and useful improvements related to carburating apparatus for the production of air gas." He received a patent March 12, 1912. Raymond and his wife, Ada O'Dowd, had one son, Herbert Victor. Raymond died in 1925.

These brothers were the first sons of Georgiana and David Alfred Doudney, who was the rector of Oid, Sussex.

Drake, Charles Flint, age 36, arrived in New York after a visit to England, September 25, 1888 with colonist E. Burlsem Thomson. They were near neighbors and joint land owners in the colony. Charles was born March 1, 1865, in Lewisham, Kent, England, to Margaret and John Drake, a produce broker. By 1901, Charles was a wine broker in London.

Dudley, (NIL)

Dunn, William H. lived in the colony by 1885. By 1891, according to Lake County deeds, William and his wife, Frances, lived in Paterson, New Jersey.

Eddes, Herbert Clement was born April 30, 1869, in Liverpool, England, to Henry and Emily Eddes. By 1881, the entire Eddes family had moved to Ontario, Canada. In 1895 Herbert married Carrie Evans in Washington, D.C., and the couple ultimately had two children, Clarence and Lawrence. After living in New London, Connecticut, where Herbert was a draftsman, they moved to Toronto, where he was an architect. He died September 11, 1929 in Pickering, Ontario. Herbert's older sister, Alice, married colonist Wilfred Western.

Elin, George Herbert Augustus, born at Lehoe House in Hertford, Hertfordshire, England, in 1864, was one of 15 children born to Dr. George and Harriet Elin. In 1883, George formed a colony social club called the Forest Club. He bought four lots in the town of Chetwynd and 60 acres in Section 5 (Lake Griffin Estate) from Stapylton. By 1893, he had returned to London, became a stockbroker, married Emma Lawrence Jacobs, and had three children, Winifred, Geoffrey and Margaretta. The family

Elin's Tandem

moved to Vancouver, British Columbia, before 1911. He died October 4, 1944, and is buried at Ipswich, Suffolk, England.

Elin, Henry Dyne, George's brother, was born in 1867. According to the Boer War website:

> He was educated at Rugby School, and has since had varied experiences in the backwoods of Queensland, the orange groves of Florida, and in Rhodesia, where he served with the Chartered Company's forces in 1890–91 during the occupation of Mashonaland. He also saw active service with Paget's Horse in the Boer War (medal), and is now a director of the Sudan Mines, Ltd. He is a keen sportsman, and especially fond of shooting, yachting, and croquet.

In 1911 Henry, unmarried and living in London, visited his brother, George, in Vancouver. But in 1925 he married the 51-year-old niece of England's Prime Minister, Neville Chamberlain. They lived at *The Gables* in Meldreth, Cambridgeshire, England, until their deaths.

Fellows, Gerald Mesey, born in 1867 in Dorset, Somerset, Wiltshire England, to the Rev. Spencer and Amelia St. George Fellows. He and Claude E. Buckle emigrated in 1886. The following year Gerald witnessed the will of G. C. Stapylton. Gerald died in June 1891 in Norfolk, England.

Foote, A. G., along with A. Merrilees and Frederick Older, ran a general store in Fruitland Park in the 1890s. A. G. may have been the same man who played in the senior singles of the Singapore YMCA tennis tournament in 1918.

Fort, U. J.

Garland, A. R.

Geary, Charles Earle McArthur, born June 2, 1856, in Kent, England, the son of Royal Navy Commander William Charles and Josephine Porter Geary. Earle, who emigrated here in 1885, was a cooperage operator in Chetwynd before moving to Leesburg where he owned and operated a livery stable. Earle married Mary Perkins (April 24, 1858–January 22, 1928) about 1886. They had two children, Evelyn Mary and Arthur Earl McArthur, both baptized at Holy Trinity. Arthur served as a 2nd lieutenant in the regular army during World War 1. Earle died April 16, 1918, in Jacksonville, Florida, and is buried at Shiloh Cemetery in Fruitland Park. He was an orange grower and a Holy Trinity founder. A sister, Helen, married colonist Reginald Cooper; another sister, Emily, married colonist Herbert Smith.

Gould, William Charles Nutcombe was born October 23, 1845, in Chudleigh, Devon, England. According to records of the British Parliament, William was a nominee for cadetship in the British Navy in 1859. He was living in the colony by 1884, when he bought 2.6 acres near the Stapylton and Company on behalf of his brother, James Nutcombe Gould, a famous British actor. William had married Ellen Raux about 1870 in Ceylon. They had one daughter, Evelyn born in 1871. The brothers were sons of the Rev. John Nutcombe and Katharine Grant Gould.

Graves, George William, listed on the manifest as "Capt. G. W. Graves, 31," George arrived in New York City on the *Egyptian Monarch* May 10, 1885, with Edward C. Windley. Their destination was noted as Florida. The 1881 English census listed him as a captain of the 1st Royal Surrey Militia. In the household was his wife, Florence, and two daughters, Sylvia and Murial. In 1887 George re-located to Murphy, North Carolina, and lived there at least five years. The *Macon County Press* described him, a retired military officer, as an "intelligent, courteous gentleman and possesses the happy tact of impressing one favorably upon first introduction, an impression that grows with acquaintance." The captain may have been a son of a London insurance broker, George Christopher, and Susanna Graves, who was born May 12, 1854.

Griffith, Charles H. E. was born in Pierrepointee, Bengal, India, November 23, 1868, to George and Charlotte Griffith. Charles and Sallie D. Ritter were married by the Rev. Joseph Julian October 9, 1889, at St. James Episcopal Church, Leesburg, and moved to Brooklyn, New York, where he was a partner in Cooper and Griffith, antique dealers, and became known internationally as an expert in antiques. In 1914 he and his family, including a daughter, Catharine, moved to Lake Sanilac, New York, where he owned an antique shop. When the Robert Lewis Stevenson Cottage opened in 1925 he not only became its curator but was an officer and director of the Stevenson Society of America. Charles died March 2, 1927.

Hale, Stuart Horsfall, according to the 1900 U.S. Census of Coconut Grove, Dade County, Florida, he emigrated to the U.S. in 1889. Born in April 1870, he was single, and a truck farmer. Stuart was the son of the Rev. Thomas and Louisa Roberts Hale of Derbyshire.

Halford, Arthur Geoffrey, born July 2, 1867, was living in the colony by 1888. By 1901 he had returned to England, where he died in Canterbury, Kent County, May 13, 1936. A 1909 ship manifest lists Arthur's marital status as "independent."

Halford, Robert Alexander born December 22, 1870, arrived in the United States with his brother and A. Merrilees aboard the *Nevada*, November 15, 1890. Robert married Fanny Emma Alexander Dunn, the daughter of Lt. Gen. E. W. Dunn, April 11, 1896, at Holy Trinity, Chetwynd, the Rev. A. Kinney Hall, officiant. Their daughter, Adria Kathleen, was baptized at Holy Trinity December 12, 1897. Her father died April 15, 1933 in Middlesex, England.

The brothers, both born in London, Middlesex, England, were sons of Charles Augustus and Geraldine Lee Dillon-Lee Halford. Through their mother, they descend from Charles I, King of Great Britain.

Hammond, J. W.

Hannah, Joseph William was born in August 1849, London, Surrey England, to Ellen and Joseph Hannah, a wine merchant. J. W., who bought 10 acres from Stapylton in 1883, was a neighbor of the Routledges on the northeast side of Zephyr Lake. A citrus grower, he was noted for tea parties and musical entertainment in his home. Never married, he emigrated here January

13, 1883, at age 36. He died August 30, 1925. His funeral was at Holy Trinity with burial at Shiloh Cemetery in Fruitland Park.

Harrington, James Henry Bowater, 23, arrived in New York June 8, 1889, aboard the *Britanic*. A son of Sydney and Elizabeth Harrington of the Bowater Estate, Woolich, Kent, England, he listed his occupation as a manufacturer on the ship's manifest. By 1918 he was listed as a claimant in Baker County, Oregon, to determine the relative rights of the waters of the Powder River. Before then he lived in San Francisco. A farmer, he married Grace Crews in LaCrosse, Oregon, and had one daughter. He died July 30, 1946, in Baker City, Oregon.

James Henry
Bowater Harrington

Harvey, Edwin John, born in September 1856, Portsea, Hampshire and married his wife, Madeleine DeFraine, in February 1885. They and their three children, Hilda, Archibald Graham Stafford, and Dorothy, arrived in the United States from Glasgow, Scotland, January 2, 1891, aboard the *Ethiopia*. Three additional children were then born: Maud, George Lancelot and a daughter, Frances Hamilton Harvey, who was baptized September 3, 1895 at Holy Trinity. Her sponsors were Robert Cowen and Maria Tatham Schrieber. Edwin was the last to purchase a lot in the town of Chetwynd. He bought Lot 5 from Kenneth Streatfield July 7, 1892. Edwin, the son of solicitor Edwin and Sarah Harvey, apparently left his wife and children and moved to Chicago, where he married Dora and practiced law.

Herford, Cyril Francis, a British subject, was born March 5, 1865, in Genoa, Italy, to Ivan Sven Herford, England's long-time ambassador to Italy, and his wife, Marion Thompson. At the Hailebury United Services College he, along with Stapylton, was a classmate of Rudyard Kipling and later a correspondent with him. Cyril emigrated December 26, 1883, and was an early partner of Stapylton and Company. He also ventured into other partnerships. In 1886 he had a half-interest in the Union Hotel in Leesburg, which included "furniture, a safe, and a kitchen range." He was also a member of the Leesburg Fire Company #1, along with F. S. A. Maude, Walter Neve and Gustav Schneider. Cyril moved to another British settlement, Rugby, located in middle Tennessee. In 1888 he entered railroad service as secretary of the Nashville and Charleston Railway and subsequently was appointed general manager. May 28 1895, he married Sadie Boyce in Lincoln, Tennessee. They had two daughters, Marion and Frances. After owning and operating a lumber business, Cyril became president of Tellico Slate and Iron Co. and was listed as a "capitalist" in the 1920 U.S. Census. He died November 9, 1950, in Athens, Tennessee.

Hervey, Arthur Cecil, son of Lt. Col. Charles and Helen Hervey, was born in 1871 in Bath, Somerset, England. He owned property near the town of Lady Lake but sold it to colonist Alfred C. Doudney in 1889. Arthur apparently never married but lived in St. Petersburg, Florida, and Bridgewater, New Hampshire while maintaining his permanent residence in Bournemouth, England. A farmer and fruit grower, he died in London May 20, 1942.

Hill, Charles H., age 22 of London, sailed on the *City of Berlin* and arrived in New York, December 8, 1884. He was enumerated in the 1885 Florida Census, living at the Stapylton and

Company boarding house. Charles was designated as the attorney-in-fact for the land sale by Capt. John Ogilby's heirs in 1891.

Hunley, E. J.

Jellicot, R. N.

Kenny, Francis Percival (January 1869–after 1930) lived in Germany before arriving in Florida about 1891. Francis, or Frank as he later became known, moved to Huntsville, Alabama, where he ran a livery. From there he took up farming in Sebera, Wyoming. Frank never married.

Kenny, Louis Lionel, born March 13, 1872, was an orange grower who registered to vote September 3, 1890. He married Hattie George (Lee) DeLong, daughter of Josiah Aikin Lee and Mary Ann Cassady, September 9, 1896, and had a daughter, Mabel Sue, who was baptized at Holy Trinity, November 12, 1904. A daughter, Mary, was born in 1902. Louis, a Fruitland Park postmaster, died in 1918 and is buried at Shiloh Cemetery, Fruitland Park.

These brothers, both born in Kirby Knowles, York, England, were the only sons of the Rev. Louis Stanhope and Arabella Elizabeth Walker Kenny.

Laugharne, H. W., born about 1863, owned Lot 32 in the Chetwynd Sub-division. At the time of the 1885 Florida Census, he lived in Stapylton's boarding house with Kenneth Streatfield, John Ogilby, G. Sutton and T. Young.

Saddle Dismount Race.
Left to Right: George Elin, Henry Elin, and H. W. Laugharne (winner).

Lemonius, Herbert Augustus, born in July 1865, Herbert was the son of merchant Augustus and Catherine MacLean Lemonius of West Derby, Lancashire. He arrived in the United States aboard the *Germanic,* March 8, 1890. He didn't stay long for he married Stella Willis in Texas, April 18,1893. An Eton College graduate, he owned a cotton yard in Galveston, Texas, when he died in 1929. In retirement, Herbert managed the Galveston Saddle Club.

Lloyd, Evan Frank, age 29, arrived in New York aboard the *Berlin* in 1888. The manifest noted that he was planning to settle in Florida. In 1894, he served as a baptismal sponsor for Cyril

Moubray, son of Arthur and Louisa Moubray, at Holy Trinity. The son of Capt. Ernest and Rosa Lloyd, he settled at the Coldstream Ranch near Vernon, British Columbia.

Long, G. C.

Love, A. G.

Lowry, Squire M. was born in 1854 in Stockport, Cheshire, Lancastershire, the son of Thomas, an engineer, and Charlotte Lowry. Squire eventually married Eliza and lived in Montgomery County, Tennessee.

Lummins, B.

Maclean, Donald Harcourt Grant bought land in the area in 1886 but accidentally shot himself while cleaning his gun at his home on Spring Lake August 28 of the same year. He is buried at Lone Oak Cemetery, Leesburg. Born September 25, 1854, in Jubbulpore, Bengal, India, he was a son of Major General John Norman Hector Grant and Eliza.

Male, George Edward lived in the colony by 1888, and sold out to fellow colonist Robert Halford in 1891. "Mr. Geo. E. Male, after spending a few months in North Carolina and Georgia, passed through Titusville, [FL] Wednesday, on his way home to Jensen." (*Indian River Advocate*, Friday, December 2, 1898.) Jensen is located near Port St. Lucie on the southeast Florida coast. A George E. Male is enumerated in the 1901 Lambeth, England census as a silversmith.

Mayo, C. R.

McLachlan R. C.

Maude, Frederick Sydney Armstrong was born November 30,1865, in Bombay, India, to Col. Edwin and Constance Wright Maude. He was educated at Eton College and Hailey-bury United Service College. In 1886 Frederick mortgaged a livestock livery stable and skating rink from J. A. Gorman that was located at the southwest corner of Lot 5 on the south side of Main Street in Leesburg. Earman Hall, located over the stable had been the site of the one of the first meetings of the new Leesburg Episcopal mission (St. James) in November 1885. In January 1887, Frederick sold a half interest to colonist W. Harris Veale who sold his interest back in a quick turn-around (see Veale below). Frederick was named a director of the Leesburg and County State Bank in 1890. As proprietors of Maude's Opera House, he and colonist Walter Neve also owned and operated a livery and feed stable, Maude and Neve's, which was located at the corner of Magnolia and Third Street in Leesburg. Their horses provided teams for road construction at the turn of the 20th century.

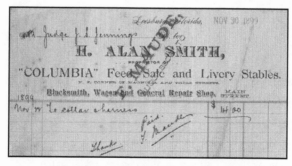

Receipt marked paid by F. Maude.

Maude served as the permanent president of the Leesburg Town Council in 1888 and as treasurer of the St. James Episcopal Church Building Committee the following year. By 1897 he was an alderman and the assistant fire chief of Leesburg. In 1902 Frederick moved to Pittsburgh while continuing as a board member of the Leesburg and County State Bank, a position he held at least until 1909. In Pittsburgh he was an exclusive agent for the Southern California Fruit Exchange that became Sunkist. After spending years in the U.S., he returned to Riverslee, Bournemouth, England, where he died December 9, 1941.

Mirrielees A., born in 1872, arrived in the United States with the Halford brothers November 15, 1890. Mirrielees, Older & Foote ran a general store that was moved from Spring Lake to the Clark building in Fruitland Park in 1890.

Mirrielees, E. J. was a member of the Bucket and Dipper Club.

These two men may be related to Albert Cazalet through the Merrielees or to the gentlemen below.

Mirrielees, Sir Frederick James, born in London and a shipbuilder there, was probably a land investor only as was his half-brother **William Spurr Mirrielees** who also owned land in Lake County.

Moubray, Arthur Rolland and his wife, Louisa Ann, arrived from Ceylon by 1888 and lived in Viola, east of Lady Lake on Lake Griffin. Four children were born in Florida: Gladys, George, Arthur, and Cyril. The latter two sons were both killed in action in France during World War 1. By 1897 this family was living in Les Pagiots, Guernsey, Channel Islands. Sometime before 1901, Arthur died. His widow earned a living as a greenhouse keeper. Arthur, a merchant, was born in Portsea, Hampshire, to George Henry and Eliza Moubray.

Muriel, Gerard Evans was born in September 7, 1860, in Norwich, Norfolk, the son of Dr. Charles and Mary Muriel. Gerard came to this country August 20, 1886, aboard the *City of Rome* with five suitcases in tow. According to Frank Cooke, "Muriel manned the hotel in Daytona" with Eugene Bosanquet. By 1895 he was living in Leesburg and listed his occupation as a traveling salesman. That same year he married Estelle Leonhart in Maury County, Tennessee, where their daughters, Sara, Gerardine and Beatrice were born. By 1910 they had moved to Jacksonville, Florida, where Gerard was a magazine editor and later an accountant. He died there March 7, 1930.

Musgrave, George, born about 1855 in Dorchester, England, arrived in the United States aboard the *Gallia* March 19, 1885.

Neve, Walter was born March 22, 1862, in Cranbrook, Kent, England, to George, a land agent and farmer of 1,190 acres, and Eliza Neve. Walter was a director of the Leesburg and County State Bank in 1890 and partnered with F. S. A. Maude in incorporating the Florida Inland Navigation Co. in 1899. By 1911 he lived in Cranbrook, Kent, England, with no occupation but "private means." He died there January 11, 1949. His brother, Frederick, a missionary Episcopal priest near Charlottesville, Virginia, occasionally served at Holy Trinity.

Nevill, Algernon Richard, was born February 1, 1866, in Ireland and emigrated to the U.S. September 7, 1888. He was the son of the Rev. Henry R. and Margaret Nevill and the husband of Maude Brierly whom he married in 1899 in England. Their son, Henry, was born in 1902. A quartermaster sergeant in the Lighthorse Division in India, he later became a tea planter there.

Nugent, G. O. In an 1888 Lake County deed of Nugent to

colonist Cyril Bonnet, Nugent is described as "G." of the Army and Navy Club of London, England, and Her Majesty's Army. Capt. G. O. was an East African planter.

Older, Frederick Charles, with Merrielees and Foote Frederick ran a general store near Spring Lake and then in Fruitland Park in the 1890s. Born April 5, 1863, and the son of Frederick Charles and Frances Beale Older, he emigrated here with his wife, Mary Hall, and son, Archibald, in 1889. Frederick and Mary sold their one acre in Fruitland Park to Walter Neve in 1892. The 1900 U.S. Census enumerates the Older family in Winthrop, Massachussetts, where they lived out their lives. Frederick was an accountant.

Ogilby, John William Henry was born October 2, 1852, in Dungiven, Derry, Ireland, to Robert and Sarah Ogilby. He was a classmate of G. C. Stapylton at Haileybury College. Following graduation he served as a captain, in the 2nd West India Regiment. By 1885 he is found in the Florida census living in Stapylton & Company's boarding house. In a letter to his father February 6, 1888, Frank Cook wrote, "Capt. Ogilby one of our colonists died rather suddenly last week from a chill caught in surveying the Race Course. He was the originator of the Races and so it seems rather hard that he should die just a week before the 1st races of the new ABC Association (American British and Colonial) of which he was President. He died at 6 a.m. and was buried at 4 p.m. [Lone Oak Cemetery]. Rather frightfully quick wasn't it?" Capt. Ogilby's siblings, David L., Mary I., Jane A. and his mother, Sarah, widow of Robert L. Ogilby of Londonderry, Ireland, sold his lots in the town of Chetwynd to Dr. Samuel Smallwood, one of the partners of the Chetwynd Land Company, March 26, 1891.

Pakenham, C.

Pybus, George Edward, the eldest son of William and Isabella Pybus, was born in July 1857, in South Stockton, Durham, England. He came to the United States aboard the *Alaska,* November 9, 1891. With him were his wife, Mary, and five of their children: Arthur, George, Percy, Mary and Eleanor. Three more children were born to them after their arrival: Gertrude, Hilda and Edmund. Edmund died August 16, 1896, at 16 days old and is buried in an unmarked grave at Holy Trinity. George Jr., 15, was the first confirmand recorded at Holy Trinity, June 21, 1896. An accountant, George grew cassava, a kind of Brazilian arrowroot, and fodder for pigs, horses, cows and chickens. Sometime after the 1900 U.S. Census, George's family moved to Atlanta, Georgia, for educational reasons. He moved there in 1902, after asking Governor William S. Jennings for a letter of reference. The governor obliged. George entered the printing business there.

Radcliffe, F. C. was a signer of the letter to the *New York Herald.*

Reynolds, Reginald Stephen, born in March 1861 in Devonshire, was buried at the Holy Trinity Churchyard, July 16, 1928. His death certificate named *Chetwynd* as the cemetery where he was buried. Before the turn of the century Stephen, who never married, had purchased the home of Josiah Aikin Lee on Lake Griffin.

Reynolds, Arthur Gerald was born in February 1862 in Appledore, Devon, England. By 1881, he was a bank clerk. Arthur "Runnels" was a bookkeeper, living in the home of J. A. and Mary Lee according to the 1885 Florida Census. Two years later he and his brother Stephen bought Lee's land in Section 10. By

1900 he was a lodger in the home of Dr. Olive Worcester in Lady Lake (Conant).

Reynolds, Edward K. was born about 1866, in Plymouth, Devon, England.

The brothers were sons of Sophie Grace and Edward Reynolds, vicar of Appledore.

Routledge, James was born October 12, 1851, at Lambeth, Surrey, England. A farmer he and his wife, Rose Jane Childley, born about 1854, arrived in the United States September 14, 1883, on the ship *Grecian Monarch*. They and their two daughters, Dorothy, born June 20, 1883, and Audrey, born September 14, 1884, both born in Florida, were enumerated in the 1885 Florida Census. A third daughter, Brenda, was born November 22, 1885. All three girls were baptized April 10, 1887, at the Vickers-Smith barn—the first Holy Trinity baptisms of record. The Routledges lived on ten acres on the northeast side of Zephyr Lake, which James purchased for $175 from his future brother-in-law, Granville C. Stapylton.

Living with the Routledges in 1885 were James' two sisters, Elizabeth, born August 20,1853, in Haggerstone, London, who married Granville Stapylton, and Harriett Susan, born January 7, 1848, Lambeth, Surry, England, who married Gustav Schneider. The acreage was sold May 6, 1895. Prior to then James managed the general store nearby. James and Rose Jane Routledge moved to Belmont, Massachusetts, near Boston by 1895 by way of Asheville, North Carolina, where Richard J. was born in July 1892. By 1920 James, a bank clerk, his wife and three daughters, moved to Needham, Massachusetts. Richard had married by then.

The Routledge siblings were the children of James Routledge and Sarah Barber.

Sergeant, Elijah B. W. was born December 1, 1863, in Walsall, Straffordshire, a son of Mary and Isaac Sergeant, a bit-maker. Elijah came to the United States in 1881 or before the colony was formed and left it about 1896. Before moving to Grenfell, Saskatchewan, Canada, he lived in Pueblo, Colorado, where he was a saddler. He is listed in Saskatchewan's *Annual Report of the Department of Agriculture* as having registered two Clydesdale horses named Redbrook and Earl of Windsor in 1904.

Schneider, Gustav Adolph, born in February 1860, in Hesse, Germany, and a civil engineer, came to the United States in 1880. He was a surveyor for the Leesburg Real Estate Association in 1886, before going to work for Morrison, Stapylton and Co., as a bank teller. About 1888 he married Harriett Routledge, born in May 1852, the sister of James Routledge and Elizabeth Stapylton, and lived in Leesburg. Gustav was the secretary of the Leesburg Fire Company #1 from 1887 through 1890. Their son, Gustav Adolph, was baptized at St. James, January 19, 1890, with Uncle Granville Stapylton, the sponsor. This family moved to Savannah, Georgia, shortly thereafter. Gustav and his son disappeared from United States public records. Harriett Schneider, however, was found in the 1910 U.S. Census as an inmate at the Georgia State Sanitarium in Milledgeville, Georgia. Although born in Germany, Gustav is listed here because of his marriage to an English woman.

Schrieber, Frederick Thomas, born December 24, 1863, in London, emigrated to the United States in 1890. By 1900 he and his family moved to Ocala, Florida, where he was a chemist and the owner of the Ocala Mining Laboratory, a consulting and analytical chemical firm. He married Maya (Maria) Tatham Turner, the niece of Emily Tatham, who donated the funds to erect Holy Trinity's lych gate, in 1889. A daughter, Emily

Dorothy, was baptized at Holy Trinity March 5, 1894, by Bishop Gray. Frederick, the son of Frederick and Elizabeth Schrieber, died January 8, 1950, in Ocala.

Sheppard, R. G. An R. Sheppard, 25, arrived in New York April 3, 1886 destined for Florida. He formed a partnership with Cyril Herford and owned a half interest in the Union Hotel, Leesburg.

Short, N. M. was a signer of the letter to the *New York Herald.* This gentleman may have been Nicholas Major Short born in 1859 in Torquay, Devon, England.

Smith, Hamilton Alan, born February 28, 1860, the son of a "landed proprietor" and fur merchant, Henry John and Margaret Marshall Smith of Muswell Hill, Middlesex. An insurance clerk prior to emigration, Alan lived in the colony by 1886 and engaged in quite a few land transactions before settling near Lady Lake where he was a vegetable truck farmer and citrus grower. Alan married Helen Waring of Montclair March 19, 1890, at St. John's, Montclair, Florida. Alan operated the Columbia Feed, Sale and Livery Stable on the corner of Magnolia and Third in Leesburg, as well as a blacksmith, wagon and general repair shop on Main Street. With their children, Eustace Hamilton and Bruce Waring, they returned to England shortly after the 1900 U.S. Census. The family was listed in the 1901 St. Mary Bourne, Hampshire, England Census—Alan "living on own means." He died May 2, 1923, in Millbrook, Cornwall, England.

Smith, Herbert of Gainesville, Florida, married Edith Geary of Fruitland Park September 2, 1891 at St. James, Leesburg. Edith was the sister of Earle Geary and of Helen Geary Cooper, wife of Reginald.

Smith, James Vickers, son of George and Jane (Vickers) Smith, was born in Stanhope, Durham, England, in 1814. He married Mary Rand February 24, 1841, in Bermondsey, Surrey, England, and by 1881, lived in London. James and Mary, along with their daughter Margaret, arrived in the British Colony in October 1884—the oldest among the settlers. Until their home on Fountain Lake was built, they lived in the Samuel F. Smith home— Samuel of Marietta, Ohio—near Fruitland Park. Daughters Sarah and Elizabeth arrived later.

The James Smith home.

A reclamation engineer—one who specializes in the art of reclaiming, embanking and draining land—his grandson, Ormond Vickers-Smith, was most proud of James' work at Portsmouth, the oldest and one of three operating bases for the British Royal Navy. In the 18th and 19th centuries major developments took place, making the Dockyard a focal point of the Industrial Revolution and in its day one of the largest centers of manufacturing, heavy engineering and shipbuilding in the world.

Also an inventor, James received a United States patent, May 4, 1886, for a combined railroad sleeper and chair. His son, John, who had arrived in the colony in May 1884, and W. G. Engleman witnessed the patent. Oddly, the patent indicates that James was a United States citizen.

The following year on December 2, James died at age 73. His was the first burial of record at Holy Trinity. Mary, his wife, died December 19, 1890, the Rev. Joseph Julian, officiant.

Of their five children, two remained in England—Helen and George, a civil engineer. All four daughters studied the art of embroidery at the Royal School of Art Needlework (now the Royal School of Art). Some of their work hangs in the shadow-boxes on the walls of Holy Trinity church, where Sarah and Margaret served as the first organists. Margaret had "full care of church" after Holy Trinity was built.

Sarah Jane (November 1842–April 11,1920), Margaret Anne (1845 Ashford, Kent, England–December 15, 1927) Elizabeth Mary (1850 St. Leonard's, Sussex, England–February 24, 1928), spinsters and farmers, lived together in the Fruitland Park area in 1920. They too are buried at Holy Trinity.

Smith, John Vickers (March 28, 1850 St. Leonard's, Sussex England–December 9,1925 of influenza) married Eleanora Thorburn Cadell (1869-1942) February 27,1894, at Holy Trinity, Chetwynd, the Rev. J. Taylor Chambers, officiant. She was a general nurse practitioner. A farmer and fruit-grower, it was John's barn near Lake Geneva that was outfitted for Holy Trinity Mission's first services.

Some time after the turn of the century the family moved

to a home on the Dixie Highway in Fruitland Park. "John Vickers Smith lost a large fine cow at his home place at Fruitland Park. The cow was feeding in a pond when a large alligator caught her by the nose, drew her head under the water and drowned her. Mr. Smith saved the cow from being eaten by the alligator, but reached the place of the struggle too late to rescue her from the saurian. " (*The Florida Star*, July 25, 1902)

Perhaps to take advantage of the increasing numbers of tourists coming to the area John and his wife opened what became known as the Park Inn in 1916. It included a general store, and had a reputation for serving excellent food.

The Park Inn, Fruitland Park, Florida.

John and Eleanor, who are both buried at Holy Trinity, had four children: Frank, Ormond, Marjorie, and Olive. Frank died February 11, 1895, at three months and is buried in an unmarked grave at Holy Trinity.

Smith, Villiers Chernocke, born November 14, 1861, in Bidenham, Bedfordshire, to the Rev. Boteler Chernocke and

Selina Sarah Couchman Smith, was a Haileybury classmate of G. C. Stapylton. After serving as a 2nd Lieutenant in the Bedfordshire militia, he emigrated to Florida in 1883. A younger brother, Charles Edward Villiers Smith, who arrived in the United States ten years prior, had already put down roots in Beaver City, Nebraska, but later became a permanent resident of Fruitland Park. Villiers is said to

Villiers Chernocke Smith

have had a very productive orange grove, the Spring Lake Grove near Spring Lake. Later he managed the 50-acre Beaman Grove on Myrtle Lake. He also served in the U.S. Army during the Spanish-American War but was not naturalized until October 16, 1906. Villiers never married.

A founder of Holy Trinity Mission, Bishop Gray appointed Villiers as senior warden in 1892—a position he held until March 1924 when he returned to Aspley Guise, Bedfordshire, England, to recover from a train accident, where he died September 9, 1925. As the third organist of record, he played the instrument for many years and sang in the choir. The Good Shepherd window above the church's altar, was given by parish members in his memory in June 1926.

Some historical accounts claim that Villiers was a cousin to the children of James and Mary Smith. That relationship has not been verified.

Soares or R. De G. Goares. The Bucket and Dipper Club membership list cites only the last name; the 1886 letter to the *New York Herald* lists Goares. More about this gentleman cannot be found.

Strachey, Claude Mainwaring was born September 1, 1861, Ashwick Grove, Somerset, England. He married Emily MacPhearson October 14, 1887, with whom he had a daughter, Olive. They then moved to Christchurch, New Zealand, where he farmed. He died in Bridgewater, England, in 1941. Their son, Pvt. Claude Strachey, born in New Zealand, was killed in action May 2, 1917, during World War I.

Strachey, Reginald Clive, born November 28, 1866, also in Ashwick Grove, lived in the colony by 1886. Clive married Anna Gibson November 6, 1893. He died April 1,1905.

These brothers were the oldest sons of a landowner and magistrate Richard Charles and Charlotte Strachey.

Stanley, Alfred and R.F.E. Cooke bought, from Villiers Smith, eight acres of land on Spring Lake in 1887, where they built a small home and several out-buildings. Alfred sold his half-interest to Cooke the following year.

Stanley, Arthur John, born 1854 London, England, to stockbroker and agent Charles and Annie Stanley, was also a stockbroker and became a solicitor after his return to England about 1888.

Stephenson, R. C.

Streatfield, Kenneth Rivers S., born April 29,1865, in Morden, Surrey, England, the oldest son of the Kent County magistrate, Alexander Streatfield and his wife, Helen McNeil. Kenneth emigrated here April 29, 1885, aboard the *Adriatic* and lived in Stapylton's boarding house with Laughorne, Ogilby, Sutton, and

Young. Kenneth served on a committee to establish Holy Trinity and was the mission's first treasurer. August 9, 1888, the Florida Produce Manufacturing Co. filed articles of incorporation with the Secretary of the State of Florida, K. R. Streatfield, president. They specialized in Seminole orange wine, orange marmalade, and golden bitters as well as French perfumes and various elixirs. A lot was purchased in the fall of 1888 but sold two years later.

Florida Produce Manufacturing Company ad.

Kenneth left the area and headed for Coldstream Ranch, Victoria, British Columbia, where he married Mabel Mary Wolfenden, the daughter of Col. Richard Wolfenden, the Queen's printer for the Province of British Columbia, in 1899. They had at least two daughters, Helen and Lorna and lived in Vernon, BC. Kenneth died there November 7, 1939.

Sutton, G. born in 1866, lived in the boarding house in 1885.

Stuart, Mary Villiers, of Waterford, Ireland.

Tatham, Emily was a Quaker who attended Holy Trinity and funded the lych gate in 1889. Born March 31, 1835, in Settle, Yorkshire, England, to Joseph and Margaret Tatham, she arrived in this country September 28, 1892, aboard the *Teutonic*. Her great-niece, Emily Dorothy Schrieber, daughter of Frederick and Maria (Turner) Schrieber, was baptized March 5, 1894, at Holy Trinity with Emily and Villiers Chernocke Smith, sponsors. She is found in the 1900 Marion County, Florida Census living with The Schriebers. Emily, a lover and defender of animals and said to have resembled Queen Victoria, died June 5, 1908, in Ocala, Florida, and is buried at the Greenwood Cemetery there.

Thomas, John Alick of London and Arthur John Stanley were involved in three land sales in Lake County with Granville Chetwynd-Stapylton in 1888. Born in 1853 in Stanstead Abbots, Herfordshire, to Louisa and John William Thomas, vicar of Stanstead, John was an architect, who specialized in designing churches, particularly in Sussex where he lived.

Thomson, Ernest Burslem, born in January 1863 in Kensington, Middlesex, England, was a Holy Trinity founder and served on the committee to establish the mission in 1886. He was the only son of Catherine Halford and William Thomson, secretary of the London Club. According to census records he emigrated to the United States in 1884 and was naturalized in 1896, about five years after his marriage to Almeida Ida Woodward, October 1, 1891, at St. James, Leesburg. A civil engineer, he helped lay out the town of Linton, Florida, in 1895 which became the city of Delray Beach. By 1900 Ernest and his wife were living in Portland, Oregon, where he became president of its Society of Civil Engineers. He was employed first by the U.S. War Department and then by the U.S. Corps of Engineers. He died in September 1942.

Topham, Harold Ward and Edwin Henry. These brothers were born in 1857 and 1858, respectively, to Dr. John and Emma

Topham of London, England. Harold, a "man of the bar," studied law at Oxford University while Edwin was an undergraduate there in 1881. They arrived November 26, 1883, in New York aboard the *Britannic*. Together they owned over 70 acres near Stapylton's Sub-division that they purchased in 1884, as well as a lot in Leesburg.

Both were seasoned mountain climbers in the Alps, the Canadian Rockies and in Alaska. Harold and Edwin, along with George Broka of Brussels, and William Williams of New York, left Sitka, Alaska, on a little schooner on July 3, 1888, and went to Mount St. Elias to climb it. They reached an altitude of 11,460 feet and then turned back. Harold read an account of this trip before the Royal Geographical Society on April 8, 1889. Both were Holy Trinity founders. Harold, who apparently never married, died May 19, 1915, in Torquay, Devon, England. Married to Adele Forget in 1889, Edwin died May 12, 1935 in Cannes, France. He was survived by two daughters, Adele and Doris.

Trimble, William Tennett was born to landowner and brewer Edward and Margaret Trimble of Dalston, Cumberland, England, in 1866. In 1886, and not yet of age, William mortgaged 40 acres on the southeast side of Lake Unity from Stapylton for $5,000 at 8 percent interest. Three years later, he sold this land to T. R. and Nancy Milam for $9,500. About the same time the Milams sold a little over 15 acres on the northeast side of Lake Harris, known as the Milam Grove, to William Trimble for $16,000. A few months later this land was sold to Edith Wingfield Pakenham, wife of Charles of Dilham, Norfolk, for 3,200 £ sterling or about $16,000. By 1891 William was back home living with his widowed mother in Dalvorson. In 1892 he, a brewer and farmer, married Frances Marion Cowen, the sister of colonist Robert Cowen, in England. They had three sons: Robert, Edward, and Stuart. For decades he served as the chairman of the board of Harrison & Hetherington, sellers of farm stock, auctioneers, brokers, and "valuers."

Trome, H. L. born about 1854, lived in the Stalpylton boarding house by June 1885.

Trower, Harold Edward was born in November 1853 in Southampton, England. He was the son of Frances and Charles Trower, a London barrister. The younger Trower, an Oxford University graduate, was also a barrister who came to Chetwynd with George S. Dawson in 1885. June 10, 1890, he married Bertha Elizabeth Schaeffer in Charleston, South Carolina. He and his wife returned to England, where he was appointed the Vice-Consul of Capri. Harold authored *The Book of Capri* which is still in circulation. He died there February 21, 1941.

Turner, Benjamin Charles Sheldon, age 21, arrived aboard the *Etruia* October 19, 1885, from Yorkshire, England, with nine pieces of luggage, remained two years and then headed northwest to Vernon, British Columbia, where he was a rancher and councilman of the newly formed town of Coldstream, where apples, pears, and hops were primary crops. He married Emma Mable with whom he had at least three children, Raymond, Hilda, and Charles, a test pilot who was killed in 1945. Sheldon died March 21, 1943, in Hertfordshire, England.

Veale, Wescott Harris Mallot was born August 23, 1864, in Franck Karle (Cape of Good Hope), South Africa to Elizabeth and Henry Mallot Harris, a wealthy landowner. January 5, 1887, Wescott married Lily Allen in Sumter County, Florida, the Rev.

John B. C. Beaubien, officiant. That same month Veale sold to his partner, Frederick Maude, for $3,000, his half-interest in a skating rink, livery stable and public hall that operated under the name of Maude and Veale, located on the corner of Palmetto and Main Street. (St. James Mission held services in the hall prior to construction of their church.)

Items conveyed included skates and repair tools, six lamps and chandeliers, 140 chairs, the drop curtains, "one horse called Crum, one called Snowball and other horses known by the following names: Roebuck, Robert the Devil, Dink, Husscoudy Maurice, and Birdie." Also single and double harnesses, two dozen whips, two dusters, eight storm aprons, two dozen halters plus one jump seat buggy, a double carriage, a double surrey, one new single buggy, six second-hand single buggies, one double hack, three double wagons, one single wagon, one sulky, one wheelbarrow, two ladies saddles, five mens' saddles, six riding bridles, one clock, "the forks, shovels, wrenches, oil, extra collars, surrey combs and other odds and ends." Office furniture and one piano were also included.

Wescott also purchased land in Lake County in 1888 and sold some of it in 1890. By then he and his wife lived in St. Augustine, Florida. Two years later Wescott and Lily of Macon Georgia, sold the remainder of their land. Wescott died in 1934 in Johannesburg, South Africa. The couple had two children: Mabel and Emily.

Vincent, Thomas Augustine T. of Dudley Vicarage, Evesham, Worcestershire, England, was born May 26, 1863, to the Rev. Thomas and Dorothea Watkins Vincent. Before emigrating here March 15, 1886, aboard the *City of Chester* he was a gunner in the Royal Marine Artillery stationed at Portsea, Hampshire, England. November 8 1893, he married Camilla Marguerite

Walker in Avondale, Duval County, Florida. They had three children: Dorothy; Augustine William, born in October 28, 1899 and baptized at Holy Trinity February 24, 1900, and Beatrice. By June 1900 this family lived in Asheville, North Carolina, where he worked as a "machine agent." From there the family moved to Monmouth, New Jersey, where Thomas was a representative of an international correspondence school. A founder and the first secretary of Holy Trinity, he died after 1930.

Union Hotel Hurdle Race, Picciola Island, March 24, 1887.
Left to right: George Elin, Thomas Vincent, and Alfred Stanley.

Weaver, Newton, born about 1865, was a farmer in the colony. An unauthored list of Lady Lake residents of this period names a Mr. Weaver who owned the "Smith shore place near Lake Sunshine."

Wetherell N. T. was born about 1848; his wife, Amy, about 1858. Although enumerated in the 1885 Florida Census, the property they owned in the area east of Zephyr Lake was fore-closed and sold to G. C. Stapylton in 1889.

Western,Wilfred Pearse P. was born September 27, 1859, in Stratford, Essex, England to Capt. (Royal Navy) Richard Roger and Jessie Pearse Western. A colonist by 1885, Wilfred had groves on Spring Lake. November 22, 1893, he married Alice Maud Eddes, a sister of colonist, Herbert Eddes, in York, Ontario, Canada, and returned to Florida. Wilfred and Alice had two sons—Eric Austin born September 11, 1895, and Hubert Upton, born February 15 1897. Both boys were baptized at Holy Trinity. By 1900 they, including a newborn daughter Vigel, were living in Asheville, North Carolina, and then moved to Toronto, Canada, in 1903 where Wilfred farmed. A Holy Trinity founder, he died in 1941.

Windley, Edward Crosland was born in 1863 in Nottingham, England, the son of Frances and William Windley, a silk throwster and cotton merchant. Edward attended Sandhurst, Royal Military College, where he starred on the rugby team. He came to Florida with Capt. Graves in 1885. Ten years later Lt. Windley was living in Rhodesia, where he was a surveyor for the British South Africa Company and later served in the West India Regiment. In 1901 he married Florence deToustain and had two sons, Rudolph and Edward. Their father Edward died April 12, 1919 in South Rhodesia.

John William Windley, Edward's brother, took over his father's company. He bought and then sold a sizable number of acres in Lake County to F. S. A. Maude for $5,000 in July 1891.

Winter, George Edward, born December 31, 1868, in Baddegama, Ceylon (Sri Lanka) to Alfred and Maria Winter, emigrated here March 30, 1886, aboard the *Egypt* and remained in the area—first living on Picciola Island and then south of Fruitland Park. A fruit farmer, he married Annie Lee, daughter of Eliza Carruthers and John Calvin Lee of Fruitland Park, March 27, 1891, at the St. James rectory, Leesburg. A daughter, Cressie, was born October 7, 1892. Naturalized October 27, 1922, George served on Holy Trinity's Vestry in 1924. He died July 18, 1928.

George Edward Winter

After the Great Freeze, George, according to family researcher Wendy Winter Garcia, grew ferns and pines for the New York market. In 1898 he, along with Frederick Schrieber, leased land in Lake and Sumter Counties that "may contain deposits of the mineral known as fuller's earth." Fuller's earth resembles clay in texture but is actually a super-absorbant, used for centuries to absorb dirt and oil. Today it is often found as a component of kitty litter. There is no evidence that this venture ever took off.

A story is told that, in 1901, George visited an aunt in England who had a pear tree in her garden that never bore fruit. George took out his knife, dug into the bark, and drew the blade all around. The next year there was a beautiful crop.

In 1917, according to his passport application, George went to Ceylon to look into the possibilities of growing rubber and going into business. Actually, he went on a around-the-world trip, funded by his older brother, Allie, that lasted at least a year and a half. While in Ceylon he grafted various kind of citrus trees at Pillagoda, one of which had 20 varieties of fruit on one tree.

According to Wendy Garcia, George was known as the "wild man of the woods," having a small steam boat which he used for fishing. He had a photograph of a large crocodile (actually it was a gator) that he had killed and stuffed, strapping it to a large basket-chair with a large straw hat on its head, and a church-warden's pipe stuck in its mouth. This picture was seen by the Rev. Charles Henry Winter, his brother, who was given the information by a clergyman (Tasker) fundraising for a church (Holy Trinity) in Fruitland Park.

One of George's hunting buddies was Frank Butler, the husband of Annie Oakley, "the peerless lady wing-shot," who shot apples off the head of her beloved black and white setter named Dave. The Butlers often visited Leesburg and stayed at the Lake View Hotel. One day Dave was killed by a car in front of the hotel. The management of Lone Oak Cemetery refused to bury him. It is reported that Dave was buried on George Winter's place, just off Montclair Road, the former home of his father-in-law, John Calvin Lee, the younger brother of Evander Lee, Leesburg's founder.

George's wife, Annie, lived on part of the old homestead until her death in 1951. Annie and George are buried at Lone Oak Cemetery, Leesburg. His sister, Sarah, married colonist Charles Newton Chesshyre.

Willis, S.H.A.V.

Winthrop, F. was a signer of the letter to the *New York Herald*.

Woodhouse, F. H. was the secretary of the Florida Produce Manufacturing Company established in Leesburg in 1888. (See K. R. Streatfield above.)

Young, T., born about 1855, lived in the company's boarding house in 1885.

Epilogue

THE FLORIDA Southern Railway Company became part of the Henry B. Plant system of railroads and steamboats in 1895. About a year later all of the 260 miles of narrow gauge track were converted to standard gauge in a single day—July 11, 1896. The Atlantic Coast line took over in 1902, and in 1967 merged with the Seaboard Air Line railroad to form the Seaboard Coast Line. Still more mergers ensued until CSX transportation took over. All railroad service to the area was abandoned by 1982 and the track removed along US Route 441/27—now nearing completion as a six-lane highway.

Stapylton's Sub-division at Lake Ella is developed with homes primarily on the east-side of the lake. The area to the east that was the proposed town of Dundee, is developed almost to US Route 441/27. Homes with large tracts of acreage and a development under construction lies to the west of *Stapylton's Sub-division* on Lake Ella Road, once called Sand Mountain Road.

Fruitland Park's southern boundary now extends to Zephyr Lake, the site of Stapylton and Company. Margaret Cooke, the widow of Frank, sold this property to P & T Company (Pringle and Turner) in 1946. The following year Pringle and Turner created the Zephyr Lake Subdivision comprised of 20 lots. Albert and Dorothy Turley bought the former Cooke-Stapylton lots, now lots 1 and 2. *The Hall* became a six unit apartment and later a bed and breakfast. Now occupying Lot 2 is the Zephyr Lake Tree Farm. Located next door on Lot 1, Frank Cooke's home, *Franmar,* is situated where Granville Stapylton's bachelor home once stood. It is privately owned and occupied.

Following Stapylton's death The Leesburg and County State Bank on 6th and Main, was incorporated as Budd and Cooke, Bankers; Hugh Budd, president and Frank Cooke, cashier. In 1907 that bank morphed into the Leesburg State Bank. Former governor, William S. Jennings, became president in 1909. Cooke became president in 1917. After acquiring the store next to the bank because of increasing business, it was decided to build a five-story bank building across Sixth Street that was completed in 1926. The original brick bank at 601 Main Street is now a boutique called Doggibags.

It took about 25 years for Lake County's citrus industry to recover after the Great Freeze(s), but it did so in a big way. From 1920 to 1983, the county was the nation's second largest producer of citrus. Miles and miles of groves could be seen all over the landscape; the fragrance of orange blossoms filled the air. But then came the freezes of 1983, 1985, and 1989. Commercial growers either gave up or moved their operations south. Today the Lakeland area in Polk County ranks number one on the list of 26 county rankings. Lake County is 14th.

For nearly 80 years Holy Trinity stood alone but tall on a hill where, to the west, one could see Spring Lake peeking through the pines. But in the early 1960s a housing development sprung up there and to the north on the shore of Lake Geneva. Although the views toward the lakes are obscure, Holy Trinity still "feels" rural.

Because of leaks, bats, and other nuisances the bell tower, that never contained a bell, was removed in 1924. Site additions since then include a parish house that contains offices and class-rooms—all anchored by a large hall, and a building for the Holy Trinity Episcopal School, a school for special needs girls and boys. A grove of oranges planted on the remainder of church's acreage in the 1960s provided additional income for the church until the severe freezes in the mid-80s.

Today Holy Trinity Church stands, not only as the spiritual home of past, present, and future saints, but symbolically as the only remaining building of a British Colony that once was—the Colony of Chetwynd.

Appendix

Bucket and Dipper Club Members
June 2, 1885–May 26, 1901

Charter Members: 19 (**bold faced**)

Back, A.
Back, G. R.
Barclay, Walter
Barclay, William
Barrett, F. A.
Barron, M.E.T.
Barrow, W. T.
Bleakley, W. H.
Bonnett, C. S.
Bosenquet, A. P.
Bosanquet, C.
Bosanquet, E. P.
Bosanquet, L.
Boswell, C. S.
Boswell, J. I.
Bovill, O. V.
Buckle, C. W.
Budd, H. S.

Cadell, J. L.
Cadell, H. N.
Cazalet, A.
Cazalet, B.
Cheshyre, C. N.
Cooke, R.F.E.
Cooper, R. H.
Cosens, F.R.S.
Cosens, S.
Coulson, G. F.
Coulson, H. N.
Cowen, R.
Creery, A.
Dawn, F.H.L.
Dawson, G. S.
Dietz, P. F.
Doudney, A. C.
Doudney, R. P.

Drake, C. F.
Dunn, W. H.
Eddes, H. C.
Elin, G.H.A.
Elin, H. D.
Fellows, M.
Foot, A. G
Fort, U. J.
Garland, A. G.
Geary, E.
Graves, G. W.
Griffith, C.H.E.
Hale, S. H.
Halford, A. G.
Halford, R. A.
Hammond, J. W.
Harrington, J.H.B.
Herford, C. F.
Hervey, A. C.
Hill, C. H.
Hunley, E. J.
Jellicot, R. N.
Kenny, F.
Kenny, L. L.
Laugharne, J. L.
Lemonius, H. B.
Lloyd, F. E.
Long, G. C.
Love, A. G.
Lowrie, S. M.
Lummins, B.
Maclean, D.G.H.

Male, G. E.
Mayo, C. A.
McLachlan R. C.
McLean, D. R.
Maude, F.S.A.
Merrilee A.
Merrielus, C. J.
Muriel, G. C.
Musgrave, G.
Neve. W.
Nevill, A. R.
Nugent, G.
Older, F. C.
Ogilby, J.W.H.
Pakenham, C.
Pybus, G. E.
Reynolds, A. G.
Reynolds, E. K.
Reynolds, R. S.
Sergeant, E.B.W.
Schrieber, F. T.
Sheppard, R. G.
Smith, H. Alan
Smith, Herbert
Smith, J. Vickers
Smith, V. C.
Soares
Stapylton, G. C.
Strackey, C. M.
Strackey, R. C.
Stanley, A.
Stephenson, R. C.

Streatfield, K. R.
Thomson, E. B.
Topham, H. W.
Topham, E. H.
Trome, H. L.
Trower, H. W.
Turner, B.C.S.
Veale, H. W.
Vincent, T. A.
Western, W. P.
Windley, E. C.
Winter, G. E.
Woodhouse, F. H.

Letter to the New York Herald,
February 16, 1886

Fruitland Park, Fla.
Settlers who are Quite Content with their Investment

To the Editor of The Herald:

The gentlemen who subscribe this protest have seen with surprise and some indignation the London telegram in your issue of the 4th inst, which reflects so unkindly, and, as we wish to assert, so unjustly on Mr. G. C. Stapylton, of Fruitland Park, Fla. We think it unnecessary to quote *in extenso* the words of your correspondent, as we know unfortunately that when a great paper gives prominence to telegrams of a damaging nature in reference to a subject which is at the time drawing considerable attention from the public, the words in question are only too likely to remain fixed and vivid before the minds of those who read.

We, the undersigned are ourselves the "enticed" of your correspondent's cablegram. We are those whom Mr. Stapylton has settled in this county of the State. We ourselves constitute the settlement, and we wish, unknown to Mr. Stapylton, to advance an emphatic denial to all that your correspondent has said in reference to the gentleman who has been instrumental in supplying us with lands on which we have created our houses.

We have not been duped; we have not been miss-led. We judged for ourselves previous to purchasing. There are among us intelligent Americans who have bought without the aid of Mr. Stapylton. We think that you will admit that not even a land agent could so far impose on some forty-five men (whose ages range from nineteen to forty) as to induce them to settle down on useless land and endeavor to make a livelihood from off it. We hope that in justice to your paper, your readers, and above all to the gentleman whose character has been maligned in your column, you will do your best to mitigate to some extent the damage which is likely to accrue to an honorable man—financial damage, not social; his friends and acquaintances still trust him. We would like above all that your commissioner could come and judge for himself, so that he might own that in this instance he had been misinformed.

G. W. GRAVES
R. CLIVE STRACHEY

PHILIP F. DIETZ
C. S. BONNETT
W. T. ALLENSON
GEO. COWAN
ROBT. COWAN
R. DE G. GOARES
E. BURSLEM THOMSON
H. ALAN SMITH
R. E. SHEL'N TURNER
F. R. S. COSENS
H. COSENS
R. H. COOPER
GEO. REID BACK
K. R. STREATFIELD
W. H. DUNN
H. W. LAUGHARNE
WILFRED WESTERN
EDWIN H. TOPHAM
F. C. RADCLIFFE
ALEX. CAZALET
B. CAZALET
N. M. SHORT
F. WINTHROP
GEORGE H. A. ELIN
V. CHERNOCKE SMITH
J. W. HANNAH
W. H. MORRISON
HAROLD W. TOPHAM
J. W. H. OGILBY
E. C. WINDLEY
ALEX. CREERY
CHARLES H. HILL

Fruitland Park, Fla. Feb. 6, 1886
Printed in the *New York Herald,* Feb. 16, 1886

Bibliography

"A Florida Bank Assigns," *New York Times*, February 12, 1895.

"A Florida Colony. Statements of a London Agent in Vindication. The Stapylton Settlement," *New York Herald*, March 26, 1886.

ancestry.com, accessed numerous times.

Bamford, Hal, "Florida History," *Great Outdoors*, 1976.

Bosanquet, Elaine and Richard, *Fair Oaks*, Leesburg Heritage Society.

Bosanquet, Dr. Louis P., electronic correspondence, 2012.

Bosanquet, Louis P., Temperature journals, University of Central Florida, MFLM F317-L2 B83.

Burke, Bernard, *A Genealogical and Heraldic Dictionary of the Landed Gentry*, Volume 2, Nabu Press, 2010.

Census of England: 1841, 1851, 1861, 1871,1881, 1891, 1901, 1911.

Census of Florida: 1885.

Census of the United States: 1880, 1900, 1910, 1920, 1930.

Chetwynd, Lake County Florida, Holy Trinity Episcopal Church, Fruitland Park, Florida, 1888.

Churchyard Records, Holy Trinity Episcopal Church, Fruitland Park, Florida.

Clarke, J. O. B., *Ocala: A Sketch of its History: Residences, Business Interests: Etc.*, Republic Press,1891.

Cohen, Kathleen Ann Frances, *Immigrants Jacksonville: A Profile of Immigrant Groups in Jacksonville, Florida, 1890–1920*, University of North Florida, 1986.

Conant, hand-drawn map of businesses and households and list of residents, 1888, Leesburg Heritage Society.

Cooke, Robert Francis Edward, letters, 1886-1894, Leesburg Heritage Society.

Coons, Michael, Personal interview, December 15, 2011.

Corporations Enrolled in the Office of the Secretary of State (Florida), online.

Davis, Dorothy Jeanne, "Florida's Bluest Monday," *Florion Grower and Rancher*, March 1958.

"Democrats of Florida," *The Weekly Florida Gazette*, Jacksonville, Florida, August 2, 1894.

Elliott, E. J., *Elliott's Florida Encyclopedia 1889*, Jacksonville, Florida.

English Colony of Fruitland Park, Sumter Co., Florida, U.S.A., Holy Trinity Episcopal Church, Fruitland Park, Florida, 1886.

familysearch.org, accessed numerous times.

fcit.usf.edu/florida/maps/galleries/state/1880–1899/index.php, accessed numerous times.

Florida Citrus; a Juicy Story, funandsun.com, 2012.

Florida Death Index, online, accessed numerous times.

Florida Semi-Tropical News, Florida International and Semi-Tropical Exposition, Inc., Ocala, Florida, January 1889.

Ford, William Wilbraham and John Rathbone, *Practical Suggestions as to Instruction in Farming in Canada and the North-west, the United States of America and Tasmania*, 13th edition, ebooksread.com, 1882.

Gannon, Michael, editor, *The New History of Florida*, University Press of Florida, 1996.

Garcia, Wendy Winter, *The Golden Falcon*, rootsweb.ancestry.com.

gillettfamily.org, Alan Chetwynd Gillett, host.

Gorgas, Major W. C., "The Results of Yellow Fever Sanitation in Havana Cuba for the Year 1901," *American Journal of Public Health,* 1902.

Gouveia, William F., *Pioneer Trails of Lake County,* self-published,1989.

"Growing Florida Towns," *New York Times,* November 30, 1885.

Haileybury College Register, 1862–1891.

Hanegen, Patrick, compiler, *Local Ghost Towns,* rootsweb.ancestry.com.

Hanft, Sheldon, "English Americans," *Gale Encyclopedia of Multicultural America,* Gale, 2000.

Hendricks, Norma, "When the English Roamed 'The Hall'," *Leesburg Commercial,* 1971, Leesburg Heritage Society.

Hendricks, Norma, "Pioneer's Grandchild Keeps Hands Creating," *Leesburg Commercial,* not dated, Leesburg Heritage Society.

Heritage Faith Challenge, Fruitland Park's Centennial, Fruitland Park, Florida, 1976.

Jackson, Rachael, "Towns That Time Forgot: Vanished Settlements," *Orlando Sentinel,* January 10, 2010.

Johnson, W. J., "A Review of Current Progress in Electricity and its Practical Applications," *Electrical World:,* Vol 18, 1891.

Journals: Diocese of Florida, 1886–1891.

Journals: Missionary Jurisdiction of Southern Florida, 1892–1915.

Kaler, F. Wilson, "The Early Days," *Florida Times Union,* August 6, 1972.

Kennedy, William T., *History of Lake County, Florida,* St. Augustine: The Record Co., 1929.

Lake County, Florida, Clerk of Court, deeds and marriages.

Lake County Florida Information: Information for the Settler and

Tourist, The Lake County Immigration Association, 1888.

Lake County, Florida, Registered Voter Lists 1894–1897.

Lake County, Florida, Tax Lists: 1888, 1890, 1895, 1900.

Lee, J. Chester, *Early History of Leesburg, Florida*, undated, Leesburg Heritage Society.

Lee, J. Chester, *The Development of the Citrus Industry Around Leesburg*, 1948, Leesburg Heritage Society.

Minutes of the Bucket and Dipper Club, Chetwynd, Florida, 1885–1901.

Mission of Holy Trinity, Chetwynd, Florida, Holy Trinity Episcopal Church, Fruitland Park, Florida, October 23, 1891.

Montifiore, Arthur, "Florida and the English," *Journal of the Manchester Geographic Society*, Vol. 5–6, p 129, May 1, 1889.

Norton, Charles Ledyard, *A Handbook of Florida*, 1891, BiblioLife, 2009.

Ocala Evening Star, January 12, 1900, September 11, 1900, April 17, 1901, January 6, 1902, February 11, 1902, July 17, 1902, October 31, 1902, May 30, 1904.

Ocala Star Banner, June 19, 1903.

Paddock, Dorothy Goodnoh, *In the Beauty of Holiness: History of Holy Trinity Church*, Holy Trinity Episcopal Church, Fruitland Park, Florida,1975.

Parish Register, Holy Trinity Episcopal Church, Fruitland Park, Florida.

Parish Register, St. James Episcopal Church, Leesburg, Florida.

"Passengers Arrived. From Liverpool, By Steamship Gallia," *New York Herald-Tribune*, November 26, 1881.

Peter, Emmett, *Lake County, Florida—a Pictorial History*, Virginia Beach, Virginia, Donning Co., 1994.

Phase I Cultural Resource Assessment Survey of the Proposed Gardenia Trail Phase II Project, Lake County, Florida, 2008.

Pozzeta, George E., "Foreign Colonies in South Florida, 1865–1910," *Tequesta: The Journal of the Historical Association of Southern Florida,* Volume 1, number 34, 1974.

Proceedings of the Eighth Annual Session of the Florida Bankers Association, online.

Raijtar, Steve, *Fruitland Park Historic Trail,* floridatrail.com.

Rast, George H. and Lee King, *My First 100 Years,* self-published, 2003.

Reaves, Louise Teague, *Conant,* no citation, Lady Lake Historical Society.

Reed, Rick, *City of Leesburg, Sesquicentennial Celebration,* Leesburg Sesquicentennial, Inc., 2007.

Reed, Rick, "Once Flourishing Communities Have Disappeared Over Time," *Leesburg Commercial,* July 22, 2003.

Reed, Rick, "Stover was an Expert on Growing of Grapes," *Leesburg Commercial,* October 18, 2009.

Reed, Rick, "The Cold Hearted Town of Conant," *Leesburg Commercial,* May 15, 2000.

Report: *Old Malden Bazaar,* Holy Trinity Episcopal Church, July, 1887.

Report of the (Florida) Secretary of State, December 31, 1888, http://ufdc.ufl.edu/.

Report of the Haileybury Natural Science Society, 1873.

Richard, John R., compiler, *Florida State Gazetteer and Business Directory, Volume 1,* New York, 1887.

Robinson, A. A., Commissioner of State Bureau of Immigration, *Florida: A Pamphlet Descriptive of its History, Topography, Climate, Soil, Resources and Statural Advantages, Prepared in the Interest of Immigration,* Tallahassee, FL, 1882.

Robison, Jim and Mark Andrews, *Flashbacks: the Story of Central Florida's Past,* Tribune Publishing, 1995.

Robison, Jim, "Decade after the Civil War was Tense, Painful for Florida," *Orlando Sentinel,* June 30, 2002.

Ruvigny, Melville Henry Messue, *The Plantegenet Roll of the Blood Royal*, Volume 2, Genealogical Publishing Company, 1994.

Service Registers, Holy Trinity Episcopal Church, Fruitland Park, Florida.

St. James Episcopal Church, Leesburg, Florida, archives.

St. John's Protestant Episcopal Church, 1888–1895, Montclair, Florida, Lake County Historical Society.

St. Paul's Catholic Church, Leesburg, Florida, Dedication Booklet, 1978.

Stapylton and Company, Articles of Partnership, December 10, 1884.

Stapylton, G. Chetwynd, letter re "The New Football," *Nation*, Volume 58 and 59, November 29, 1894.

Stover, Loren, "100 Years of Cotton Growing in Central Florida," *Orlando Sentinel Star*, November 18, 1951.

Sumter County, Florida, deeds.

Sumter County, Florida, plat maps.

The City of Fruitland Park, Florida, Today 2001, compiled by Maria J. Schofield.

The London Standard, classified, London, England, May 22, 1884.

The Morning Post, classified, London, England, January 8, 1886.

Tischendorg, Alfred P., *Florida and the British Investor: 1880–1884*, Alfred P. Tischendorf Papers, University Archives, Duke University, 1970.

University of Florida Digital Collections, accessed numerous times.

uscemeteryproj.com/florida/lake/lake.htm, accessed numerous times.

Untitled document re Chetwynd and Sand Mountain Road by unknown author, dated before 1956, Leesburg Heritage Society.

Valentine, Doris, *Looking Back, Sumter County*, Sundial Print Shop, 1981.

Vestry Minutes, Holy Trinity Episcopal Church, Fruitland Park, Florida.

Vickers-Smith, Lillian, *The History of Fruitland Park, Florida*, 1924.

Warnke, James R., *Ghost Towns of Florida*, Star Publishing Company; 3rd edition, 1971.

Will and estate papers, Granville Chetwynd-Stapylton, Lake County Probate Records.

Williams, Clarence R., *Aunt Bob's Book*, self-published, 1945.

Williams, Clarence R., *Life with Gertrude*, self-published, 1948.

Wysong, Elsie Baylor, *History of Sumter County, Florida*, self-published, 1993.

About the Author

T HOSE WHO know D.R.S. Bott call her Bott or Bottsky; a few dare to call her Donna. Whimsy led her to adopt the common British three-initial moniker as a tribute to the ladies and gentlemen of the Colony of Chetwynd. She got to know most of them well over the past four years while writing *The Chetwynd Chronicles*. In fact, Bott has become the leading expert of all things Chetwynd.

D.R.S. Bott

Born in Canton, Ohio, the cradle of professional football, her education, interests and passions led her into the worlds of music, business, genealogy, historical research and writing.

Before the coming of the internet Bott and her husband, Larry, arranged most of their vacations around pertinent court-houses or they sequestered themselves in local libraries as part of her quest to seek long-forgotten ancestors. As a result she privately published *Diggin' in Granny's Root Cellar*.

Grace Episcopal Church, Morganton, North Carolina, published Bott's *Amazing Grace* in 1997—an extensive history of the church's first 150 years. While researching and writing *The Chetwynd Chronicles* she also researched for *Coming Home*, authored by Ivan Ford, the history of Holy Trinity Episcopal Church, Fruitland Park, Florida.

Lest you think that Bott spends all of her waking hours investigating other people's pasts, she really doesn't. Her passion for golf led her, by then a widow with four cats, to The Villages, Florida, where one can ". . . play golf free for the rest of your life." She plays and plays often. But beware. Except during half-time, please don't bother her during football season. It's in her genes.

Visit with D.R.S. Bott at thechetwyndchronicles.com or contact her at thechetwyndchronicles@gmail.com.

Made in the USA
Charleston, SC
04 April 2013